PRAISE FOR
Lives of American Women

"Finally! The majority of students—by which I mean women—will have the opportunity to read biographies of women from our nation's past. (Men can read them too, of course!) The Lives of American Women series features an eclectic collection of books, readily accessible to students who will be able to see the contributions of women in many fields over the course of our history. Long overdue, these books will be a valuable resource for teachers, students, and the public at large."

—COKIE ROBERTS,
author of *Founding Mothers* and *Ladies of Liberty*

"Just what any professor wants: books that will intrigue, inform, and fascinate students! These short, readable biographies of American women—specifically designed for classroom use—give instructors an appealing new option to assign to their history students."

—MARY BETH NORTON,
Mary Donlon Alger Professor of American History,
Cornell University

"For educators keen to include women in the American story, but hampered by the lack of thoughtful, concise scholarship, here comes Lives of American Women, embracing Abigail Adams's counsel to John—'remember the ladies.' And high time, too!"

—LESLEY S. HERRMANN,
Executive Director, The Gilder Lehrman
Institute of American History

"Students both in the general survey course and in specialized offerings like my course on U.S. women's history can get a great understanding of an era from a short biography. Learning a lot about a single but complex character really helps to deepen appreciation of what women's lives were like in the past."

—PATRICIA CLINE COHEN,
University of California, Santa Barbara

D1592819

"Biographies are, indeed, back. Not only will students read them, biographies provide an easy way to demonstrate particularly important historical themes or ideas. . . . Undergraduate readers will be challenged to think more deeply about what it means to be a woman, citizen, and political actor. . . . I am eager to use this in my undergraduate survey and specialty course."

—JENNIFER THIGPEN,
Washington State University, Pullman

"These books are, above all, fascinating stories that will engage and inspire readers. They offer a glimpse into the lives of key women in history who either defied tradition or who successfully maneuvered in a man's world to make an impact. The stories of these vital contributors to American history deliver just the right formula for instructors looking to provide a more complicated and nuanced view of history."

—ROSANNE LICHATIN,
2005 Gilder Lehrman Preserve American History
Teacher of the Year

"The Lives of American Women authors raise all of the big issues I want my classes to confront—and deftly fold their arguments into riveting narratives that maintain students' excitement."

—WOODY HOLTON,
author of *Abigail Adams*

Lives of American Women

Carol Berkin, Series Editor

Westview Press is pleased to launch Lives of American Women. Selected and edited by renowned women's historian Carol Berkin, these brief, affordably priced biographies are designed for use in undergraduate courses. Rather than a comprehensive approach, each biography focuses instead on a particular aspect of a woman's life that is emblematic of her time, or which made her a pivotal figure in the era. The emphasis is on a "good read," featuring accessible writing and compelling narratives, without sacrificing sound scholarship and academic integrity. Primary sources at the end of each biography reveal the subject's perspective in her own words. Study Questions and an Annotated Bibliography support the student reader.

Barbara Egger Lennon

Teacher, Mother, Activist

TINA STEWART BRAKEBILL

Illinois State University

LIVES OF AMERICAN WOMEN
Carol Berkin, Series Editor

WESTVIEW PRESS

A Member of the Perseus Books Group

WESTVIEW PRESS was founded in 1975 in Boulder, Colorado, by notable publisher and intellectual Fred Praeger. Westview Press continues to publish scholarly titles and high-quality undergraduate- and graduate-level textbooks in core social science disciplines. With books developed, written, and edited with the needs of serious nonfiction readers, professors, and students in mind, Westview Press honors its long history of publishing books that matter.

Copyright © 2014 by Westview Press
Published by Westview Press,
A Member of the Perseus Books Group

Find us on the World Wide Web at www.westviewpress.com.

Every effort has been made to secure required permissions for all text, images, maps, and other art reprinted in this volume.

Westview Press books are available at special discounts for bulk purchases in the United States by corporations, institutions, and other organizations. For more information, please contact the Special Markets Department at the Perseus Books Group, 2300 Chestnut Street, Suite 200, Philadelphia, PA 19103, or call (800) 810-4145, ext. 5000, or e-mail special.markets@perseusbooks.com.

Series design by Brent Wilcox

A CIP catalog record for the print version of this book is available from the Library of Congress
ISBN 978-0-8133-4771-4 (paperback)
ISBN 978-0-8133-4772-1 (e-book)

10 9 8 7 6 5 4 3 2 1

CONTENTS

Contents

SERIES EDITOR'S FOREWORD

For the past half century, American historians have focused much of their work on writing ordinary people into the national story. "History from the bottom up" was a recognition that our past is shaped not simply by the famous and powerful; it is created by the choices made by the majority of women and men. Often, their lives help us understand the major changes, the critical events, and the conflicts of their era. This is true of the long life of Barbara Egger Lennon, which began in the 1880s, as industrialization and urbanization, along with a great wave of immigration, created the modern era, and which ended almost one hundred years later, in what many call postmodern America. As Tina Stewart Brakebill shows us in *Barbara Egger Lennon: Teacher, Mother, Activist,* Lennon's personal evolution coincided with dramatic changes in assumptions about gender roles, work conditions, and education. Lennon was not a passive observer of these changes; she embodied them. As Brakebill explains, this Swiss immigrant from a traditional farming family took full advantage of new opportunities that presented themselves to young women. She pursued a college education when this was rare for women; she became a school principal when few women were promoted from the classroom; she became an outspoken and effective union organizer, a full-time working mother, and a social and political activist in reform causes. Brakebill's observation is true: Barbara Egger Lennon was multitasking before this term became a commonplace description of the challenge of women's lives.

Lennon's long and active life provides a window onto a broad sweep of American history: from Reconstruction to labor organization, to the Great Depression, through two world wars, through progressive moments such as the New Deal and anxious moments of the Red Scare and the Cold War. Sometimes these historical events seem too abstract, but their complexities and their stark realities come alive when we can see them played out in an individual life.

Brakebill offers us a beautifully drawn portrait of a remarkable woman of achievement. Not every reform battle Lennon engaged in met with success, of course, and not every personal relationship turned out as she might have hoped. But Lennon refused to be a passive observer of history. Instead, she chose to shape her world whenever the opportunity arose. The legacy of women like Barbara Egger Lennon is the wealth of opportunity enjoyed by American women today.

In examining and narrating the lives of women both famous and obscure, Westview Press's Lives of American Women series populates our national past more fully and more richly. Each story told is that not simply of an individual but of the era in which she lived, the events in which she participated, and the experiences she shared with her contemporaries. Some of these women will be familiar to the reader; others may not appear at all in the history books that often focus on the powerful, the brilliant, or the privileged. But each of these women is worth knowing. American history comes alive through their personal odysseys.

—*Carol Berkin*

ACKNOWLEDGMENTS

This project followed along a circuitous path to completion, and its success would have been impossible without a lot of support. Space precludes listing everyone, but some people merit special recognition. The staff at the McLean County History Museum (MCHM) is foremost on that list. Executive director Greg Koos gets credit for "introducing" Barbara Egger Lennon to me nearly a decade ago. Once I was able to commence research in earnest, MCHM head librarian and archivist Bill Kemp and archivist George Perkins stepped to the forefront. Throughout the multiyear research process, they both offered consistent help and encouragement. Fellow archival researchers will understand the comfort of being on a friendly first-name basis with a competent and knowledgeable library and archives staff who will always respond to a last-minute e-mail. Simply put: my gratitude for Bill and George is vast.

Thank you to my editors, present and past, for believing this project had merit and for helping to turn an idea into words on the page. Neither this book nor the Lives of American Women series would exist without the hard work of Carolyn Sobczak, Catherine Craddock, Ada Fung, Carol Berkin, and Priscilla McGeehon. Annette Wenda's fantastic copyediting skills deserve high praise as well. I also must acknowledge the encouragement offered by another group of women, my women's writing group—Women Historians at Middle Illinois—with special thanks to several of the group's members. Ignoring my apprehensions that my subject was too unknown to be included in such a prestigious series, Stacy Cordery strongly encouraged me to submit a proposal and then provided very helpful feedback on my proposal draft. Eliminating my fear of the "cold call," Stacey Robertson offered electronic introductions to the Lives of American Women series editors and served as a commiseration partner when we temporarily lost its press. Plus, as a good friend, she offered sisterhood when I needed a morale boost. Throughout the process, Monica Cousins Noraian has provided steady reinforcement, reminding me that I am capable of great things and that chocolate is a magical cure. And finally, a big thanks to Sandra Harmon. She has read drafts of almost everything I have ever written, and this project was no different. Her input is invaluable.

Throughout this process, I continued teaching at Illinois State University, and, likely unbeknownst to them, my students imparted many valuable lessons along the way. I am especially grateful for their energizing presence. My friends and colleagues at Illinois State University also offered encouragement and an empathetic sounding board when needed. But, as Barbara Egger Lennon's life so aptly illustrates, multitasking can be challenging. As an adjunct professor, scholarship is not an expected duty, so I carve research and writing time out of my nights, weekends, spring breaks, holidays, and summers. Striving to meet my varied professional goals has often meant that I don't see the people I love as much as I'd like, and when I do see them I am exhausted. But because they appreciate the passion I have for teaching, research, and writing, they rarely complain. I fear naming names in case I miss someone, but I hope you know who you are and how much having you in my life means to me. I would be remiss, however, if I failed to mention the one person who lives with the chaos on a daily basis. Brian Brakebill has loved and believed in me longer than I have loved or believed in myself. Thank you for all the days gone by, and let's go on choosing each other for all the days to come.

Introduction

Barbara Egger Lennon (Barbe) lived a long life. She was born in the early 1880s and died in the early 1980s. Innumerable changes characterized this hundred-year span. She witnessed the transition from horse and buggy and dirt trails to the automobile and the Eisenhower highway system and beyond. When she entered high school, the manual typewriter qualified as advanced office technology, and by the time of her death, the first personal computers had made their way into home offices all across the nation. She began teaching seventeen years before women gained the right of national suffrage, and by the time she retired in 1950 her political activism had garnered invitations to the Illinois Governor's Mansion and the White House. Her personal and professional evolution occurred alongside the transformation of American culture from nineteenth-century traditional to twentieth-century modern. But simply living through change does not mean a person's life merits further historical interpretation. So what makes an unknown woman like Barbara Egger Lennon worthy of study?

At first glance, her life seems pretty ordinary for a white midwestern woman of her time. She was a daughter and then a teacher before becoming a wife, a mother, and then a widow, a life path common at the time. What complicates that assumption of ordinary is that she also was a college student, a school principal, a union organizer, a social and political activist, and a full-time working mother, activities less common for women at this time. Even less customary was the fact that for the greater part of fifty years, she engaged in many of these ordinary and not-so-ordinary activities simultaneously. Throughout the first half of the twentieth century, Barbe constantly reshuffled her priorities as she attempted to balance these varied facets of her life. Her evolution from a deferential student and then teacher with a high school diploma to a college-educated professional educator to union organizer and political activist illustrates women's changing presence in the public sphere. At the same time, her path from daughter to wife to mother offers a picture of the more static reality of assumptions regarding women's family responsibilities. Her efforts to be a "good" mother, employee, and citizen required the sort of multitasking common for twenty-first-century women, but her story certainly complicates traditional views of women's lives before the 1970s. When she died in 1983, she left behind a son and six grandchildren, but she also left behind roles as an educator, union organizer, and political activist. This book examines the path that produced that varied legacy and provides new details to enrich the growing tapestry of women's history.

As an author and historian, enriching that tapestry with the stories of seemingly ordinary women is my passion. But knowing that Barbe's story should be told did not guarantee it could be told. Gathering sufficient evidence about the lives of nonfamous women often proves difficult. Luckily, Barbe also left behind a documentary legacy. For more than sixty years, she kept a journal in which she noted the events of her daily life. Over the years she also put together scrapbooks full of ephemera connected to public activities. In truth, however, many women keep daily journals and scrapbooks commemorating what they thought important, but the vast majority of these pieces of history never end up in an archive. For far too long, women's lives were considered, at best, tangential to history and important only as they connected to men's stories. As a result, records documenting women's everyday family lives, such as diaries, letters, and scrapbooks, commonly end up lost or discarded or forgotten in a family attic. Barbe's connection to a male labor activist (John Brown Lennon) and the MCHM's commitment to local stories saved her written legacy from that possible fate. The continued existence of this treasure trove provided the raw material necessary in order to unravel the individual threads of her life and reweave them with broader historical trends in order to illuminate not just Barbe's life but also the challenges many women faced in the first half of the twentieth century. What follows are the results of that effort.

NOTE ON NAMES

In academic writing common practice dictates the use of last names once a person has been introduced into a narrative. Biographical writing, however, often complicates that tradition. It is not practical to use only last names when subjects are married couples or family members with the same last name. Furthermore, if a woman changes her last name after marriage (and in the middle of the story), then those standard naming practices can be confusing to the reader. Some writers solve this latter potential problem by using last names for men and first names for women, but this overfamiliarity toward women (and not men) tends to reduce women to secondary figures and seems unnecessarily dismissive to women. To avoid confusion and maintain respect for the subject of this biography, first names are used for all members of both the Egger and the Lennon families (once they have been initially introduced with their full names). Other people (male and female) are introduced by their full names and then referred to either by their full names or by their last names depending on which usage is less confusing.

1

From Student to Teacher, 1880s–1902

On the evening of June 18, 1900, fire broke out in the central Illinois community of Bloomington. Helped by a brisk wind, the fire spread through the mostly wood-frame structures simply too quickly for the fire equipment of the day. Fortunately, the conflagration claimed no lives, but by the next morning the largely uninsured downtown business center laid in waste. Rather than succumb in despair, Bloomington citizens chose to tackle the tragedy as an opportunity. One of the city's businessman boosters said it best: Bloomington would "rise again . . . greater than ever."[1] Rebuilding began almost immediately, and by the next summer twentieth-century designs of brick and stone had begun to replace the ruined remains of the nineteenth.

While the rise of modern structures proceeded as planned, new starts proved harder for those without insurance or deep pockets, and these unrecoverable losses could have unforeseen consequences. For high school student Barbara Egger (Barbe), the fire ultimately changed her life's path. She had been boarding with a local cigar manufacturer who lost his uninsured business to the fire and his home to the financial aftermath. His disaster left Barbe potentially homeless until another local couple, Juna and John Brown (J. B.) Lennon, brought Barbe into their Mulberry Street home. This move was Barbe's third major relocation in her young life, and although it was the shortest in distance, its effects were significant. The couple apparently intended to provide temporary shelter for a displaced girl in exchange for household help, but Barbe soon became a part of the Lennon family. The Lennons assumed the role of surrogate parents in a way that her boarding family had not. This surrogacy changed her life as well as theirs.

But before their paths could intertwine, they had to find themselves in the same place, and this process spanned several decades and two continents. Seventeen years earlier, while still a toddler, Barbe took her first step toward this meeting when she left her hometown of Thal in the canton of St. Gallen, Switzerland.[2] Under the sole guidance of her mother, Barbara Katherine Toggler Egger (Katherine), Barbe and her five siblings (aged infant to teen) set sail from Le Havre, France, on the steam ship *La Normandie* along with a thousand other third-class passengers en route to America. After an arduous three-week transatlantic trip, they landed at Castle Garden in New York in June 1883. This exhausting trek was followed by a series of trains that took them another thousand miles, nearly halfway across the country, to their final destination of Odell in Livingston County, Illinois. It was there that the family reunited with Barbe's father, Jacob Egger. He had made the journey approximately a year prior to his wife and children and had already settled among the many other immigrants populating the northern Illinois farming community. Jacob's desire to preserve a long-established way of life inspired him to move his family halfway around the world; ultimately, however, this first move set Barbe on a path that led away from the presumed traditional life of early marriage and farming and toward change.

This change had begun with the intersection of the sweeping social trends of industrialization, urbanization, and modernization. By the early 1880s, the Industrial Revolution had transformed St. Gallen's traditional embroidery work from a local craft enmeshed within an agricultural base to a booming industrial export business. These new economic opportunities brought wealth to the region, but some farmers, including Jacob, viewed the accompanying social and cultural shifts with fear. The desire to avoid the upheaval of industrial change and protect a simpler, more traditional way of life had pushed him to leave St. Gallen sometime in 1882 in search of a new place to reestablish an old way of life. Luckily, like many of the 25 million immigrants who endured transatlantic voyages and cross-country treks in the decades between the Civil War and the Great War, he had a path to follow. Letters from kin, friends, and community members served as ready advertisements for the possibilities and challenges of a new place. These missives and return visits from earlier travelers lent an aura of familiarity to a foreign locale and fueled migration chains in which newcomers followed the paths laid by their migrating predecessors.

For the Eggers, this chain led to Illinois, where industrialization, urbanization, and modernization had also brought tremendous change and growth. In 1850 fewer than one hundred miles of railways had existed, but by 1860, thanks to large federal land grants, twenty-six hundred miles transected and connected the state. One of the most important rail expansions extended from Chicago to St. Louis. This line opened up outlets for industrial and farm products and helped to give birth and growth to Illinois communities such as Odell in Livingston County and Bloomington in McLean County. This boom provided thousands upon thousands of jobs building, maintaining, and running the lines while also creating access to millions of acres of cultivable land. In order to sell this land and lure cheap labor, the rail companies, land speculators, and the federal government advertised and recruited aggressively among new arrivals in the United States as well as sending agents to Europe to attract possible emigrants. In Illinois German and Irish immigrants grabbed up many of these jobs and acres, but in 1858 a St. Gallen emigrant planted the first roots of what would become a small but thriving Swiss contingent nestled among these other European transplants in Livingston County.

By the time the Egger family arrived, this initial St. Gallen transplant had produced a small network of Swiss immigrant families who, like their mostly Irish and German Livingston County neighbors, had settled into traditional farm community life. The Egger clan quickly did the same. By the early 1890s, the family had grown to include ten children, three boys and seven girls. Despite the desires of many immigrant fathers, America often offered their daughters and granddaughters a chance at a life governed less by the restrictive "Old World" ideas about women's narrowly prescribed roles. Nonetheless, these shifts were less common in rural settings than in urban environments, and this certainly seemed true for the Egger family. Barbe, her sisters, and her mother shared in the duties traditional for farm women such as caring for the animals, milking the cows, and churning the butter. In addition, the women took care of other traditionally female work such as cleaning, cooking, canning, sewing, and laundry. For Barbe's sisters, these same roles continued into their adult lives. Four of them married farmers at a young age, while the youngest surviving daughter continued her traditionally supportive duties at home. (The last of the ten children—a daughter born in 1892—died in 1897.) Only Barbe's experience strayed from this traditional pattern of early marriage, multiple children, and a life of farming. Ironically, this divergent life path was made possible by the very industrial forces and societal shifts the Eggers had sought to escape.

Like Barbe's father, many native-born Americans feared the myriad effects of the changing times. But for a significant number, rising immigration was the most troubling aspect of these changes. They anxiously watched as Thomas Jefferson's ideal agrarian republic gave way to a modern, urban, industrial landscape largely populated by wage-laboring immigrants who seemed unfamiliar with core American ideals. Reactions to this perceived problem ranged from immigration restrictions and nativist violence to aggressive "Americanization" programs. Within the context of the latter, educational reformers stepped forward and successfully emphasized the role schools could play in preparing young people to participate "appropriately" in the American social order. In the late nineteenth century, this belief that the school should both drill students on the "three R's" and instill American values led to the vast growth of a tax-supported educational system in which universal and centralized institutions taught a shared curriculum to all students regardless of their background—in short, "public" schools.

Public schools were not new. By 1860 all thirty-four states had adopted laws requiring tax-supported public schooling. Yet considerable disagreements existed over how universal institutions and a common curriculum should be defined and implemented. The result was an incomplete and fragmented system. In the decades after the Civil War, however, those fears regarding the changing industrial world accelerated the school movement, and new state- (and county-) level regulations brought universal public education closer to reality. By the 1890s the length of both the school day and the term became more standardized, and many states, including Illinois, mandated compulsory attendance for children under fourteen. As a result, between 1880 and 1900, Illinois student enrollment and daily attendance dramatically increased. Extensive school construction and renovation also moved Illinois communities gradually away from one-room schools to larger brick and frame structures. Despite this growing emphasis on the role of education, reformers believed that for most children, primary-age schools provided sufficient training to instill the necessary skills and values to participate in American society. As a result, education beyond the eighth grade was still rare. Illinois had only three hundred high schools, and in 1900 only about 5 percent of all eligible students nationwide entered high school, and the majority did not stay to graduate. While this number signified quite an improvement over the 2 percent level of 1870, high school was still far from the norm.

Barbe became one of those small numbers when she graduated from high school in 1902. The motives for this path are unclear, as Barbe's education set her apart and marked her as the odd member of her family. A family dynamic may explain her desire to escape the Egger farm. Her father, she later confessed, was rarely sober and treated the family "like dogs." She placed the blame for her mother's unhappy and troubled life squarely on her father's uneven temperament. His drinking sometimes led to violence. "Pa acting so terribly. Lost a valuable horse simply because he struck its head with an iron rod." Her father's overbearing demeanor and selfish attitude left scars as well. She once lamented about her own childhood, "I am not responsible for being restrained in every way the first fourteen years of my life and so am or feel timid or backward about asking for things or being communicative."[3] Reflections such as these suggest an unhappy childhood, but was this enough to explain her path?

Given her status within the traditional household and her self-proclaimed timidity, the choice probably was not hers to make as a teenager. Economic factors were probably at play. The farm was small, the family was large, and in 1896 (when she moved out) the economy was still in the midst of the depression produced by the panic of 1893. Her older brothers soon moved west, looking (in what would be a failed attempt) to strike it rich, but that still left eight children at home, seven of them girls. Large farm families like the Eggers commonly expected their unmarried daughters to boost family income or, at least, pay their own way until marriage by taking advantage of the new teaching opportunities created by the expansion of the public school system. With her older sister's marriage on the horizon, Barbe (as the second oldest daughter) was the next logical choice for this strategy. Relocating fifty miles southwest to Bloomington also made sense, as it offered access to an excellent school district known for its teacher preparatory work.

This reputation was no accident. In 1892 the city's first female school superintendent, Sarah Raymond, ended a nearly twenty-five-year career in Bloomington during which she spearheaded a vast revisioning of public schools. Under her watch the city built more schools, improved existing facilities and materials, hired and promoted qualified teachers, standardized the curriculum, and won certification for the high school. Whether students planned only to complete their required eighth grade education or, like Barbe, intended to move on to high school, Bloomington's nine public grade schools offered a solid foundation. And in October 1896, Barbe made her second major move when she left Odell and relocated to Bloomington, where she entered seventh grade at Jefferson grade school. She struggled initially with the more advanced curriculum but quickly found her footing. In eighth grade she earned "Excellent" scores in all her subjects. She even won a one-dollar prize in a local patriotic essay contest. After successfully completing eighth grade, gaining entry into Bloomington High School (BHS) became her next challenge. This step required scoring at least a 75 percent on a comprehensive exam. She accomplished this task and in September 1898 became one of the few students throughout the nation entering high school. True to Bloomington's stellar reputation, BHS was one of the few Illinois high schools requiring a four-year program for graduation, and students faced a challenging curriculum. In Barbe's class of 1902, only 44 graduates emerged from the total first-year enrollment of 432 students. Barbe proved worthy of her chosen curriculum, which included Latin, German, Botany, Physics, Chemistry, Geometry, History, Rhetoric, and English. She pursued her studies diligently and was excelling academically when the aftermath of the Bloomington fire brought the Lennons into her life.

This meeting was somewhat serendipitous, as J. B. and Juna Lennon's path to Bloomington also was not a direct one. J. B. had been born in Wisconsin in 1849. His mother proudly claimed her place in the Daughters of the American Revolution (DAR) as the daughter of a former Revolutionary War officer. His father's American lineage was not as long, but he had emigrated from Manchester, England, as a child. Not long after J. B.'s birth, the family moved to Hannibal, Missouri, where his father established a tailoring business amid the tensions that eventually took the nation into civil war. Missouri had long played a significant role in this tension. In 1820 the Missouri Compromise had brought it into the Union as a slave state, and Hannibal's port was an active slave-transporting hub. Slave ownership also was common. During the 1850s, however, German immigrants and migrants from the North and East, like the Lennons, introduced a strong strain of antislavery sentiment to the state. These opposing forces as well as its position as a border slave state complicated things further when it came time to take sides during the Civil War. Ultimately, the state chose not to secede, but many people remained strongly proslavery.

The Lennon family's actions during this period made their allegiance clear and helped cement a lifelong commitment to progressive reform in young J. B. In addition to her proud DAR heritage, J. B.'s mother was a somewhat distant cousin to the infamous abolitionist John Brown. The Lennons may not have condoned Brown's participation in the violent murder of five proslavery men in "Bleeding

Kansas" or actively supported his attempts to foment war at Harpers Ferry, yet they were self-described abolitionists. At one point, according to family history, they risked prison or worse by harboring a group of runaway slaves in their home. Whether this family lore was completely truthful is unknown, but its inclusion in various news items commemorating J. B.'s mother's death in 1906 illustrates the importance the family attached to their commitment to the antislavery movement. As another measure of this commitment, within months of the war's outbreak J. B.'s father enlisted in the Union army, where he spent the next three years.

The family weathered the war years, and once the fighting ceased J. B.'s father resumed his tailoring trade. As a testament to the family's progressive leanings, he did not insist his now sixteen-year-old son take up the trade. Instead, he supported J. B.'s desire to attend Oberlin College in Ohio, which was one of the earliest institutions of higher learning that accepted both women and African Americans as students. He managed to spend seven months in this progressive hub before economics forced his return to Hannibal. In hopes of a better future, the entire family relocated in 1871 to booming Colorado. J. B. initially dabbled in mining and farming but ultimately joined his father's tailoring trade. This decision prompted his lifelong association with the labor movement. He helped organize Denver's first central labor council, represented the city's tailors, and was elected to national leadership positions in the Journeyman Tailors Union (JTU) and the American Federation of Labor (AFL). His commitment to labor activism took him to New York City in 1886 and then to Bloomington, Illinois, in 1894. Once permanently settled in that up-and-coming labor hub, he became a central figure in local labor concerns while also maintaining his national prominence and connections with the AFL and the tailors union. He even relocated the JTU's national headquarters to Bloomington.

By the time Barbe moved in with the Lennons, J. B. had a long history as a respected labor reformer and a public advocate for progressive causes such as women's suffrage and temperance. Juna, however, was still in the early years of what also would be a very successful tenure as an active public reformer. Little is known about Juna (Allen)

Lennon's early life. Born in 1849, she and her family lived in New York and then Vermont before relocating to Hannibal soon after the Civil War ended. In 1871 she and J. B. married, and soon the entire Lennon clan moved to Denver. She gave birth in 1873 to the couple's only child, a son named John Frank Lennon, and devoted the next twenty years to motherhood. The 1894 relocation from New York to Bloomington offered a change, as her now twenty-one-year-old son did not accompany the family west. The couple's move also coincided with the advent of the "Progressive Era." This period of social and political activism celebrated modernization but also worked to counter the negative effects of industrialization and urbanization. Although not all progressives agreed on the problems, or the solutions, the reforming fever offered women increased opportunities for public involvement. By the late nineteenth century, middle-class female reformers had pushed the boundaries of what many viewed as women's acceptable sphere of influence outward. Using traditional ideas about women as their justification, these "social housekeepers" claimed the right to be involved in any facet of society that potentially affected women or children or the safety of the family. After her arrival in Illinois, Juna took full advantage of this wider sphere by supporting the women's suffrage movement as well as becoming actively involved in a variety of social reform groups.

It was one of these social reform connections that brought the newly homeless Barbe together with the Lennons. This third move in Barbe's short life had both immediate and long-term consequences for all three. As a couple the Lennons offered Barbe a model for Progressive Era activism, and this left an important impression on her. The fire and the dislocation could have put an end to her school days, but instead their home allowed her the space to spread her wings during her final two years of high school. Her scrapbooks, which she began soon after moving in with the Lennons, are filled with mementos of dances, parties, games, and plays. She also pasted clippings documenting Juna's extensive club and volunteer activities and J. B.'s work. The interest seemed mutual. Juna stepped in as a surrogate mother and hosted Barbe's social and school functions at their home. J. B.'s work often took him out of town, but he sent notes that revealed his affection and his respect for Barbe's intelligence. For example, during one lecture trip, he sent her a copy of the speech he gave to the Illinois Federation of Women's Clubs, entitled "The Industrial Problem as It Effects [*sic*] Women & Children." His esteem for her intellectual capacity was not misplaced. She continued to earn high marks in all her classes and display excellence in other endeavors. In the spring of 1902, Barbe won top honors in an open essay contest based on the writings of renowned international travel writer John L. Stoddard. She treasured her prize, an eleven-volume illustrated set of travel discourses on Europe, Asia, and the Middle East, which offered a fascinating window into a wide variety of exotic locales. With this success behind her, she embarked on the final months of school and her proudest high school accomplishment: becoming the editor in chief of Bloomington High School's monthly newspaper, the *Aegis.*

The need, desire, or opportunity for work meant that boys waived the noncompulsory chance at a high school education in far larger number than girls. So at BHS, like most high schools of the time, young women made up the majority of students. Despite this fact, the *Aegis* staff was overwhelmingly male. Barbe's assigned status as editor in chief testified to the administration's belief in her abilities. Her first issue of the newspaper contained a sixteen-page retrospective of the city's successful postfire rebuilding efforts and a two-page editorial section covering topics ranging from curricular changes to the assassination of President William McKinley. The issue, visually attractive and well written, did not go unnoticed. An article in the *Chicago Chronicle,* which focused on the "Model School System in Bloomington," noted that the school's monthly newspaper was one of its "most praiseworthy products." Barbe herself received glowing praise: "Miss Egger's literary productions show remarkable talent and she may attain fame as a writer."[4] Other school newspapers also regularly critiqued and validated her work. Barbe's undeniable pride is evident in the twenty-seven positive reviews she pasted in her scrapbook. The *Chronicle* article had speculated on a future writing career for Barbe; nevertheless, an assumption made by one reviewer is a reminder of the narrow socially acceptable roles for women. This reviewer suggested that the author of an *Aegis* story look more carefully at some of the statements he made. Barbe also pasted this review in her scrapbook, but she circled the *he* in dark ink, clearly taking offense at the assumption of male authorship.

The presumption that the editor was male tells us much about how slowly gender ideals changed. Barbe was about to graduate into a world that still defined women's acceptable public participation very narrowly. Most women still worked only out of economic need, and by 1900 women still made up less than 20 percent of the total labor force, concentrated mostly in domestic or factory wage labor. Professional opportunities were few and dominated by the so-called female professions of teaching, social work, and nursing, for these drew upon the nurturing character believed to be natural in women. Barbe was well aware of societal and family expectations regarding her future, and her BHS program of study was designed with a teaching path in mind. As graduation approached, Barbe began a job search armed with that pragmatic goal. The competition would be intense, for the presence of two nearby universities made it possible for local school boards to set high standards. They expected first-year teachers to have either completed a two-year college-level teaching course or successfully taught for three or four years in an outside school.

Barbe countered this policy by offering proof of an excellent high school record and several strong letters of recommendation. One letter concluded with the sentiment that she was "a young woman of strong character, good scholarship and good sense. She has the power to do what she undertakes and I am sure that she will succeed as a teacher." A Bloomington business owner and former street commissioner wrote directly to the McLean County school superintendent, introducing Barbe as "a personal friend of the family . . . capable of fulfilling any position." He closed his recommendation by noting that "any favor shown her will be appreciated by your friend." On April, 26, 1902, J. B. also wrote directly to the superintendent and expressed "Miss Barbara Egger's desire" for a school as close to Bloomington as possible. Any help in this matter, he added, would be considered "a very great personal favor." These efforts on her behalf were successful. On May 30, 1902, Barbe received the news that she had been chosen unanimously out of eight applicants for a position at the Eldorado

School, a county school on the outskirts of the Bloomington city limits.[5] Less than a week after this notification, she graduated third in her class of forty-four students. Barbe's high school career was now over. The next week the local paper noted that her future plans included teaching for one year before going to college. Ambitious words, but she likely knew them to be ultimately unrealistic. She no doubt understood that graduation had set the stage for what was expected, not what was wished.

2

Personal and Professional Deference to Authority, 1902–1908

When Barbe stepped in front of her first class in 1902, she still may have hoped to enter college in a year's time, but that goal proved untenable. Instead, after two years at Eldorado, she moved to a slightly larger school thirty miles west of Bloomington in Hopedale, Illinois. Unlike the one-room schoolhouses that still dominated rural districts, Hopedale offered separation by grades. She now taught only fourth grade and no longer had to worry about disciplining seventh or eighth grade students only a few years her junior who sometimes towered over her barely five feet of height and 110 pounds. The distance from Bloomington also meant that during the week, she boarded in Hopedale. The Lennons still attempted to oversee from a distance, but this shift offered her first real taste of limited independence. Nineteenth-century norms had mandated nearly constant familial supervision and gender-segregated activities, but the twentieth century brought change. The twentysomething crowd in Hopedale spent much of their free time together in mixed-gender unsupervised, or at least minimally supervised, groups. They picnicked and played tennis during good weather and went ice skating and sleigh riding and had snowball fights during the winter months. But these group activities also offered opportunities for couples to form, and that dynamic provided a reminder that shifting norms did not negate the assumed limits of female autonomy in 1905. Barbe originally may have hoped to pursue higher education after a short stint at teaching, but her hints of a hopeful romance reveal that she perhaps, like society, now presumed a different goal. Marriage continued to be the expected and most frequently traveled path for women, and it was certainly all around her. Over the next decade, she collected a steady stream of marriage announcements and consistently made note of upcoming weddings in her journal. In the first nine months of 1905 alone, at least six of her friends married, including one of her closest confidantes, fellow BHS class of 1902 graduate Myrtle Selby.

The early twentieth century offered women slightly expanded professional and personal opportunities, such as teaching, but society still tended to view these opportunities as merely an interlude between student and wife. And the pomp leading up to the Selby wedding certainly provides a glimpse into the importance still attached to the presumed ultimate goal of womanhood: marriage. In the two weeks prior to Selby's ceremony, the local newspaper detailed various aspects of the prewedding rituals on at least ten separate occasions. Barbe also described each event and pasted memorabilia connected to these festivities in her scrapbook. As the wedding day approached, she attended a linen shower, a variety shower, and a kitchen shower, as well as hosting a china shower. Like most things, she took this responsibility very seriously. She decorated the Lennons' house with wildflowers she personally gathered, prepared the food, and sent out hand-drawn invitations to a least eighteen people, which included a verse she also wrote: "Myrtle Selby is going to wed! On the eight of September, Miss Egger has said—I wish you to bring her a cup or a plate. So please remember to be there by eight. I use the word plate 'cause it rhymes with eight, but I mean any china by piece or by crate. So here's to the Houses of Selby and Shannon! The shower to be given at the Home of the Lennon's."[1] To her pride, the shower was a great success, and a few days later she witnessed her friend's entry into wedlock. That same week, Barbe's life also shifted, but not because she had found a husband or finally entered college. Instead, she left Hopedale and returned to Bloomington.

The Hopedale School Board had wanted Barbe to return as a teacher in the fall of 1905, but she also received an offer from the Bloomington School Board. Hopedale certainly had its attractions, but other considerations complicated the decision, and her eventual choice of Bloomington was a function of both personal and professional realities. Beginning in the nineteenth century, communities increasingly turned to women to fill the growing need for teachers that accompanied the rising number of schools. Both ideology and pragmatism fed this trend. Widely held beliefs defined a woman as naturally nurturing and submissive. These traits made her a perfect substitute mother in a classroom of young children, but they also made her a perfect employee to serve under the mostly male school boards and administrators. Hiring women also made fiscal sense to school boards answering to taxpayers. Female teachers could be paid significantly less money than male teachers simply because they were women. Like most teachers, Barbe's experience was affected by both the ideas about and the realities of being a female teacher. She struggled to live up to the middle-class standards communities expected from female teachers while earning a working-class wage. Despite significant cost inflation and a move to a bigger school, her salary had risen only from forty to forty-five dollars per month in the past three years, and the twelve-dollar monthly boarding cost dug deep into this small sum. Many teachers solved this problem by continuing, or returning, to live with family, so the Lennons' free room and board clearly offered a financial incentive. But even if frugality is set aside, emotion also exerted a strong sway. Over the previous five years, Barbe had transferred much of her feelings of familial obligation and affection from her birth parents to the Lennons. Quite simply, the Lennons had offered her a home and changed her life. It proved difficult to ignore their wishes that she return to Bloomington.

Those emotional ties did not mean, however, that Barbe was firmly committed to the idea of leaving Hopedale. From all indications, she had been happy and enjoyed her expanded sense of autonomy. She had established a network of friends and colleagues, a friendly rapport with her boarding family, and perhaps a possible prospect for a long-term relationship. She also enjoyed her students and had a good working association with the Hopedale School Board. Her succinct journal note following the news that Bloomington had offered her a job spoke volumes about her conflicted feelings: "Rcd [received] letter from home saying I had been chosen as a teacher. Not over happy about it."[2] She hesitated to give up the short-lived sense of (albeit still limited) independence Hopedale had provided. The same week as that job offer, J. B. and Juna arrived in Hopedale for a visit. Discussion about the decision must have taken place during the Lennons' daylong stay. This probable discussion was followed two days later with a missive from J. B. about her school choice. The exact content does not survive of either the conversation or the letter, but only a few days later the decision had been made, and it reflected the Lennons' wishes. On the fifteenth of May, the Bloomington School Board issued its official teaching appointments for the fall of 1905, which included Barbe's assignment as a fifth grade teacher. In June she moved back to Bloomington permanently and continued her teaching career in the same place where her years as a Bloomington student began, Jefferson School. This move led to a shift away from autonomy and toward deference in both her personal and professional lives that would prove difficult to alter.

Professionally, Barbe's reentry into the Bloomington school system began at a point when ideas about the ultimate purpose of schooling were again evolving. By the late nineteenth century, the notion that schools should instill American values as well as impart basic skills was firmly established. By the early twentieth century, many progressive reformers had expanded these goals in an attempt to incorporate the perceived pragmatic needs of the twentieth-century industrial nation. In the years to come, the mantra of "practical education" would serve as shorthand for promoting an educational agenda that envisioned different roles for men and women in this new world. Nineteenth-century educational reforms had drawn more women into teaching, and by the early twentieth century women significantly outnumbered men not only as teachers but also as students in high schools. To practical education proponents, this imbalance represented a threat to the success of a business-centered future. Harbingers of this danger could be found everywhere. A local school newsletter warned that current educational policies lacked appreciation for practical things. This supposed lacuna led boys to quit school and ambitious men to leave teaching, thus abandoning the schools to women. A few years later, an Illinois school superintendent summed up the supposed danger of these female-dominated schools. "She [a female teacher] can inspire him [the male student] but she cannot correct his wrong habits as well as a man. . . . She cannot take the place of a man." His belief echoed the thoughts of many reformers. Women's assumed maternal patience was perfect for grade school teachers, but once students reached the higher grades they needed the disciplined directives only male teachers could provide. By 1914 this fear that women teachers "feminized manhood [and] no woman, whatever her ability, is able to bring up properly a man child" had earned a name equal to its hyperbole: "The Woman Peril in American Education."[3]

So how could the United States avoid this "peril"? Reformers offered a broad range of ideas designed to retain boys as students and men as teachers while also providing a context for what many in society viewed as a properly developed manhood. Schools needed to offer more practical courses, pay men higher salaries than their female counterparts, raise men's overall salaries, and provide male teachers better opportunities for advancement. This progressive style of "scientific" school management, as it was quickly labeled, moved the nation's high schools away from a narrow focus on nongendered college preparation to an emphasis on real-world and gender-separated courses intended to prepare for life without college. Now boys took commercial and manual training classes, and girls took domestic arts and sciences classes. But these gendered shifts also reached beyond the student body to the organizational structure of many school systems. As the twentieth century unfolded, men increasingly dominated the growing number of higher-paying administrative and high school teaching positions; women, while still the majority in numbers, overwhelmingly served as teachers in the lower-paying and less prestigious grade school positions. Grade school teacher autonomy also was reduced, as school boards increasingly mandated almost every facet of the curriculum. By the time Barbe returned to Bloomington as a teacher, the school district had enthusiastically embraced these progressive ideas. The board had added manual training and domestic arts classes to the curriculum and adopted a new style of administration known as "horizontal supervision."

Despite the moniker of "horizontal," hierarchy was the defining element of this system. At the top was the school board, which hired the head administrator, or superintendent. Beneath the superintendent were various supervisors who assisted the superintendent in administrating the system. The superintendent was in charge of the high school's direct supervision, but a supervisor administered the grammar grades (one through four) and a different supervisor oversaw the primary grades (five through eight). Other individual supervisors took charge of various subject areas, such as music, physical culture, domestic science, penmanship, and drawing and handwork. These supervisors regulated the classroom teachers in their handling of their particular subject areas and circulated through the schools, giving lessons to every room every two weeks. Beneath them were the individual schools' teaching principals, who taught full schedules while also attending to the everyday oversight of their schools. Prior to this time, principals had been strictly supervisory positions, but the switch to the less authoritative (and lower-paid) teaching principals resulted in their quick conversion from male- to female-dominated positions. They lacked the same level of authority, status, and salary as supervising principals, but they did provide women slightly increased pay, autonomy, and access to educational leadership, and thus they were potentially empowering facets of a rather rigid gender construct. Finally, beneath the teaching principals were the classroom teachers. Salaries reflected gendered hierarchy as well. Barbe's pay slowly rose after she returned to Bloomington, but almost ten years later she (and her fellow female grade school teachers) earned only $75 per month for a nine-month contract. This annual pay of $675 was about 75 percent of the average pay of male downstate grade school teachers and was dwarfed by the $3,500 paid per year to the Bloomington school superintendent, which for more than one hundred years after Sarah Raymond's resignation was not held again by a woman. In the fall of

1905, Barbe entered the Bloomington school system at the bottom rung of this hierarchical ladder at a salary of just over $400 per year.

The morning after she had hosted Myrtle Selby's successful wedding shower, Barbe began her Bloomington teaching career by attending her first of many teachers meetings. She listened dutifully as her superintendent reinforced everyone's designated responsibilities on the eve of the new school year. After the conclusion of this mandatory Saturday-morning meeting, the entire family (Barbe and both Lennons) took the train to Chicago for a weekend of fun that included the opera, the theater, and a citywide automobile tour, the latter still being a very novel event. Then early Monday morning, she took her place at the head of her class of thirty-five fifth grade students, and the memory of the Windy City weekend quickly faded as she endeavored to fulfill her duties as outlined in the Bloomington School Board's *Rules of the Public Schools.* Standards dictated everything from the temperature of the classroom and the required use of a flexible instrument for corporal punishment to the mass of data needed for the numerous required reports. The "rules" also contained detailed curricular plans for each grade, outlining what, how, and when every subject was to be taught as well as the specific books and materials to be used. Teachers were not allowed to vary this program or materials, so very quickly a routine was established.

Barbe oversaw the curriculum as detailed by the school board, led the class in lessons provided by supervisors, graded assignments and exams provided by supervisors or the superintendent, and attended mandatory meetings held by the superintendent, her various supervisors, the Teachers and Patrons Club, and the Mothers Club (the latter two served as early versions of what would become the Parent-Teacher Association). She also spent considerable time preparing the required weekly and monthly reports detailing students' attendance, behavior, tardiness, and progress. Most reports, although tedious, were straightforward, but progress reports could be complicated. She did not have complete autonomy over student scores, and the principal or superintendent commonly instructed teachers to either mark low or not grade too high. The superintendent also had the final word on whether a student should be promoted. In addition, although Barbe was responsible for day-to-day instruction, her principal, the various subject-area supervisors, and the superintendent were a consistent, albeit varied, presence in the classroom. Sometimes they merely observed, sometimes they taught, and other times they provided direction for their particular subject. Occasionally, Barbe revealed impatience with this facet of "horizontal supervision." Subject supervisors received higher salaries than teachers, so she thought it unfair that they often expected teachers to lead the class in their specialized topics instead of teaching it themselves. This complaint reveals an early streak of private defiance, but even the local teachers' professional support organization, the Central Illinois Teachers Association, was headed by administrators, so avenues for grievances were mostly nonexistent. So, for the most part, she acquiesced quietly to the dictates of the various school authority figures.

She also struggled, not always successfully, to gain a sense of control over her students. Bloomington city youths seemed considerably more unruly than the farm children of rural Hopedale. She, as well as other teachers and supervisory officials, commonly employed corporal punishment as discipline for infractions. Deliberately incomplete work, rowdy behavior, or impudence could result in whipping or slapping students with a ruler or hose, both of which complied with the flexible-instrument rule. But the use of discipline did not always result in the desired attitude change (in the teacher or student), and nearly two months after starting she still struggled. In late October 1905, she grumbled, "Children mean—fairly hate my school. Monotonous life." This mind-set extended into the holiday season, and she dreaded her return to the classroom. But, to her surprise, she found things improved, as the students behaved better. This attitude adjustment stuck, and in May 1906 when Hopedale once again tried to lure her back, she said no with regret but also confidence. "Feel as if I would like to accept but know that I would never be satisfied after teaching here in town. Have found this year's work very hard but trust next year's will be easier." This prediction largely was accurate. Dealing with students, parents, and school officials continued to offer challenges, but she settled into a routine that reflected the consistency and adherence to protocol that the school board endeavored to establish. This attitude helped to ensure her continued employment, as each summer teachers essentially had to be rehired for the upcoming school year.[4]

Adjusting to a new work environment was not the only change in Barbe's life. The return to full-time residence in Bloomington also altered her social life. Initially, Barbe took the lead in trying to build a network of peers. She brought together twelve women—married and single former classmates, fellow teachers, and friends—and helped organize a social club dubbed the "A Volonte Club." As the club's first president, she helped plan the gatherings, which in that first year could be quite elaborate. They staged a "stag" party, where they all dressed as men, drank grape juice, and "smoked" candy cigars and pipes. In contrast to that theme was the "spinster" party, where they dressed as their favorite unmarried fictional female character and shared the story of why their chosen subject had never married. Unlike the stag party, Barbe chose not to dress the part for this gathering, claiming exhaustion. No doubt she was tired, but she also might have struggled to celebrate spinsterhood, as one by one she watched her friends and colleagues marry, while she remained single. Their twice-monthly gatherings did not always adhere to themes; sometimes they simply had tea and cake. They did, however, continue to offer the somewhat rare chance to socialize outside the context that quickly dominated her social life: her role as the Lennons' surrogate daughter.

This role could be somewhat less festive. For example, Juna brought her into a women's group known as the Mosaic Circle. Rather than being simply a social club, members undertook a rigorous nine-month schedule of lectures and debates on a variety of topics. Each season culminated with an imaginary trip through a chosen region. In 1906 each member took the group on a virtual tour of a region in South America. The couple sometimes also included her with their friends in the Twentieth-Century Euchre Club, which met regularly to play cards. Even when no organized club events were scheduled, evenings and weekends were seldom empty. During good weather, a long horse-and-buggy ride was a favorite after-dinner pastime, and in the winter the buggy shifted to a sleigh. The house would not have a Victrola record player until the early 1910s (or a radio until 1929), but the family enjoyed wide access to a variety of live musical, and nonmusical, performances. The nearby Illinois State Normal University as well as numerous downtown Bloomington venues offered myriad concerts, plays, and a wide variety of visiting speakers. Plus by 1908, the downtown Columbia Theater also played ten-cent "moving-picture shows." Bloomington's downtown business association also sponsored special events. Barbe was an avid window-shopper, so she especially enjoyed the "style show" each spring. People crowded around the stores in the darkness, and then all the businesses simultaneously brought their lights up to reveal store windows decorated using live models. In the summer, a merchants' boat parade brought thousands to Miller Park Lake for the annual "Venetian Night." Regardless of the entertainment value of these many options, her role was as the Lennons' surrogate daughter. This dynamic meant that many facets of her social life mirrored the patterns of deference endemic to her work life. This pattern also extended to her household responsibilities.

One of the pulls of Bloomington had been the fact that she did not have to pay room or board. Nonetheless, she did take on (what she often decried was more than) her fair share of the labor needed to keep the household running. Barbe sewed most of her own clothes, mended family garments, swept and mopped floors, wiped down woodwork, cleaned the stove, cooked meals, baked breads and sweets, planted and maintained vegetable and flower gardens, canned vegetables, jammed fruits, did the laundry, and ironed. According to Barbe, Juna rarely helped with these many chores, as she was either claiming to be ill or off volunteering. Not surprisingly, Barbe also often complained about the monotony and drudgery of the housework, which still felt decidedly nineteenth century. For example, she washed the laundry in a tub with a hand-operated wringer and then hung it on a line to dry. Cleaning the many rugs also remained virtually unchanged. She first swept the rug by hand and then picked it up and beat it to remove more dirt. By 1908 a newly available compressed-air cleaner offered potential relief for the latter task, but the motorized tool cost a dollar per day to rent and required two men to operate. After trying it once, Barbe convinced Juna that the sheer amount of dirt it sucked up made it worth the money. For several years, the family rented this tool every three or four months. Then in 1911, Juna purchased a more advanced canister-style Justrite vacuum for twenty-five dollars. Its advertisements boasted, "You don't have to take a bath or shampoo after using. . . . One person can operate it. You can clean the whole house before dumping."[5] But new technology can have potential disadvantages as well. Vacuum cleaners raised acceptable cleanliness standards while also putting the chore squarely back in female hands. In the Lennon home, the "one person to operate it" invariably was Barbe, so its touted time-saving advantage was up for debate.

To make matters worse, Barbe also felt that Juna lacked appreciation for her efforts, especially given that Barbe also worked outside the home. This assumption contributed to the sometimes uneven relationship between the three household members. J. B. traveled frequently as part of his JTU and AFL duties and as a popular national temperance speaker. His frequent absences left space to miss him, his work gave Barbe much to admire, and his lack of day-to-day household authority diminished potential resentment. So not surprisingly, when he left on any of his many trips, she could lament his absence. Their relationship continued to display the affection and admiration evident during her high school years. On the rare occasions when he and Barbe were home and Juna was absent, the two got along well. For example, in April 1906, Juna spent a week in Washington, DC, as a DAR delegate. While she was away, J. B. and Barbe enjoyed horse-and-buggy rides, uptown walks, and occasionally dinners out at one of the many downtown restaurants. Barbe and Juna never achieved this ease of companionship, and whether J. B. was home or away the two women struggled to define their relationship, especially after Barbe's return home in 1905.

Once Barbe settled back in Bloomington, this mother-daughter dynamic reached a critical juncture as they tried to adjust. Juna had been Barbe's most consistent parental presence since 1900, and, in some ways, Barbe appreciated her motherly interference. After the father of one of Barbe's students spoke harshly to her, Juna intervened. She contacted him and, according to Barbe, "called him to time—told him he wasn't a gentleman. Said I could neither put brains nor

character in his children." Juna intervened again when the Bloomington School Board moved Barbe to another school against her wishes.
Juna rallied students and parents to write letters in Barbe's favor and
request that the reassignment be reversed. The effort failed, but Barbe
had happily allowed Juna to take the lead in this campaign. More
often than not, however, Barbe privately complained about Juna's attitude and expectations. In May 1906, just one year after moving back
to Bloomington from Hopedale and only weeks after Juna's DAR trip,
Barbe summed up her fear and frustrations: "[Juna] said a number of
cutting things. I don't know what to do. I think the world of her and
try to please her, but do not succeed. I feel as if no one cared a snap
about me and that I am in the way everywhere." Barbe never openly
defied Juna about anything significant, but she believed that Juna
went out of her way to find fault. Two years after Barbe's return, the
tensions had worsened further. In October 1907, as Barbe described
it, Juna subjected Barbe to a "tirade of abuse" and accused her of being "sly and unreliable." Juna ended this tirade by warning Barbe that
she had "better find a different home," because "they didn't always
want me along."[6]

Myriad reasons likely contributed to the friction, but clearly their
struggles were connected, at least on some level, to the fact that both
women coveted J. B.'s time. If Barbe's reporting is at all accurate, then
Juna felt possessive of her husband's attention. When possible she attempted to carve out time for the couple by taking private buggy rides
or retreating to their private upstairs rooms. Barbe often complained
that she felt excluded by Juna's slights and resented what she described
as Juna's selfishness. As for J. B., he very rarely took any sort of definitive stand; instead, he usually chose to stay on the sidelines. When
time came to plan for the annual AFL convention in 1907, he did just
that. Barbe had accompanied the couple to every convention since
1901, but when Barbe asked about their plans he was noncommittal.
He did not directly invite her, nor did he clearly tell her she was not
invited. She and Juna fought about a number of petty things throughout that week, but Juna never clearly declared Barbe unwelcome either. Instead, when convention time came, Barbe opted to stay home.
Despite the fact that neither J. B. nor Juna had explicitly invited or

disinvited her, she privately blamed only Juna for the fact that she was left behind. After the couple left, Barbe spent a day crying herself almost sick and the next two weeks dwelling on Juna's attitude.

After the Lennons returned home from this trip, the tensions did not disappear, but a temporary change in routine altered the context of their issues. In December 1907, famed evangelical preacher Billy Sunday arrived to much fanfare and stayed in Bloomington for more than a month. In his first four days alone, he spoke to more than eighteen thousand people at six different events. Some attendees, no doubt, watched Sunday for entertainment alone, but both Juna and J. B. were swept away by the Sunday evangelical fever. The couple rarely missed any of his many sermons, and they "came forward" at one of Sunday's services to announce their intentions to pledge their lives to evangelical Christianity. Barbe, on the other hand, was resistant to Billy Sunday's influence. In part, no doubt, this was because his arrival coincided with her worst tensions with Juna, who was clearly enraptured with Sunday. The couple struck up a friendly relationship with him, and Barbe resented the time Juna devoted to Sunday. Typical complaints included Barbe's grousing that Juna had time to bake a cake for Billy Sunday yet never had time to help with the housework. But Barbe also felt slighted by her belief that Juna did not want her to join the First Presbyterian Church with the Lennons. These hurt feelings clearly connected to her insecurities regarding Juna's feelings, because Barbe failed to be convinced by Sunday's brand of religious practice.

She did not disagree with all his stances. Like Sunday, she supported temperance, the end of child labor, and female suffrage rights, but she failed to see the logic of the mandates to stop dancing or theatergoing or card playing. She privately questioned what good came of the Lennons' withdrawal from the Twentieth-Century Euchre Club, if it meant damaging an old friendship. Sunday also lambasted the Unitarians as non-Christians, and Barbe definitively disagreed with this position. Before Sunday's arrival, the family had not attended any one church regularly, but of the several they did visit Barbe found the Unitarian Church the most appealing. Its emphasis on emulating Jesus by living a good and upright life and its welcoming attitude spoke to her in a way that Sunday's somewhat dogmatic rules and talk of eternal damnation did not. Once the Lennons embraced Sunday's style of evangelical teachings, Barbe feared Juna's objections, so she kept her thoughts to herself and avoided going to the Unitarian church regularly. This period of spiritual self-examination did, however, lay the foundation for her eventual choice to join the Unitarian Church.

Once Reverend Sunday left town, the two women's constant bickering seemed to slow to occasional outbursts. Based on Barbe's oft-mentioned fear that she was "pushing in," however, she retained lingering doubt and resentment regarding her perceived status in the house. In June 1908, her doctor attributed her recurring headaches, weight loss (she had dropped to 99 pounds), and insomnia to worry and prescribed wine before dinner as well as calomel pills. The wine is ironic, considering the household's temperance advocacy, but calomel (a mercury-based drug) as a supposed cure for both physical and emotional issues was dangerous. Its poisonous qualities actually caused additional health problems that plagued Barbe over the next few years, including hair loss and the deterioration of her teeth. In the midst of her ongoing health issues, one of those occasional flareups resulted in Juna's accusations that Barbe was "selfish . . . and did very little work . . . and should find another *boarding* place."[7] And in November 1908, she once again missed the annual AFL convention because, according to Barbe, Juna told her directly that the couple did not want her along.

Barbe's continued feelings that the Lennons considered her only a boarder reflected her fear that Juna would deny her place as a family member. Nonetheless, despite Barbe's anxieties and Juna's outbursts, Juna and J. B. clearly viewed Barbe as more than a boarder. She spent every summer and holiday break with them rather than her birth family, even accompanying the Lennons to Denver in the summer of 1907 for a family reunion. And from an outsider's view, even the friction between Juna and Barbe offered a not uncommon dynamic between a newly adult daughter and mother. So even given their continuing contentious interactions, it is not entirely surprising that Juna and Barbe's relationship provided a foundation for Barbe's eventual growth in confidence and independence. In short, even though

Barbe's admiration for J. B. had been more obvious and consistent, Juna's social and political engagement provided the example Barbe first emulated and then eventually expanded upon as her sense of self-worth grew.

The opportunity to actively act on this example first occurred in the early summer of 1908. After months of tension between the two women, Juna reached out and asked Barbe to join her in the local fight to curb the sale of alcohol. Thanks in large part to the work of the Women's Christian Temperance Union (WCTU), support for prohibition was growing. As a result of this groundswell, the Illinois Legislature passed a law in 1907 allowing precincts to vote on a "local option" to control the sale of alcohol. In the spring of 1908, the local Anti-Saloon League succeeded in getting an initiative to close all saloons on the Bloomington ballot. The group was careful to emphasize that this vote was not an attempt to control what a man drank in his own home; rather, it was meant to protect Bloomington families from the crimes and lost wages so closely linked to drinking establishments. To demonstrate their support for this position, Barbe and Juna marched, along with more than twenty-three hundred women and children, the WCTU, and the Boys Temperance Brigade, in an antisaloon parade. Banning saloons was a softer line than complete prohibition, and many other communities in Illinois voted yes on similar options. But even this tact had stiff opponents in Bloomington, especially among union working men. The local option failed to find sufficient local support, and the "wets" defeated the "dries" by a wide margin. Even though their ultimate cause failed this time, this effort marked the first subtle shift away from Juna as solely a familial authority figure to a more cooperative working relationship, albeit one still characterized by hierarchy. Their collaboration must have inspired Juna, because only two weeks later she once again included Barbe. This time the goal was to organize a Bloomington branch of the Young Women's Christian Association (YWCA).

The YWCA first appeared in large urban areas in the late nineteenth century to provide aid to the increasing number of young, single working women living away from home. By 1908 the YWCA had become a hallmark of social housekeeping women's efforts to help working women. Similar to the boardinghouse movement, its middle-class female proponents envisioned the YWCA as a pocket of morality providing matronly guidance and refuge from the corruption of single city life. By the early twentieth century, the YWCA had grown into a nationwide system of associations devoted to "the Spiritual, Intellectual, Social, and Physical development of all young women." Membership in the Bloomington branch was available to "any women of good moral character" who could pay the one-dollar annual fee.[8] The steps that led to this Bloomington refuge began on April 20, 1908, when Juna and other local women met informally to talk about bringing a YWCA to Bloomington. A week after this discussion, Juna requested that Barbe join her at the first official organizing meeting.

Over the next few months, Barbe aggressively participated in the campaign to gain the pledges needed to make their local branch a reality. She went door to door, spoke to church groups, and reached out to friends and colleagues. She kept a running tally in her journal and proudly bragged when her pledge total was the highest, which was often the case. Once sufficient money was pledged, the women incorporated the organization. The new group appointed Juna to the Board of Directors, and the board elected her treasurer. Based on her pledge prowess, Barbe was made the chair of the Membership Committee and given the power to assemble her own committee workers. She reached out to downtown female store clerks as her first line of workers, and membership quickly swelled. By June 1908, the newly formed YWCA had secured rooms downtown, served its first healthy dinners to downtown working women, and opened a "restroom" to provide a safe respite for working women. This project was the first time Barbe took a relatively autonomous role in a reform effort. It raised her confidence level, and its success helped lay the groundwork necessary for the further activism and greater career autonomy that lay in her future.

3

Aspiring New Woman, 1909–1915

Barbe's journey toward greater autonomy took place during the sweeping changes that characterized the early-twentieth-century Progressive Era. Women, in particular, unleashed their potential and power to alter the status quo. The battle for female suffrage intensified, female-centered social and labor reform organizations grew in size and influence, single working women increased in numbers and social acceptance, women's access to higher education widened, and perceptions about women's appropriate private and public roles shifted. Women did not always agree on their specific goals or on the best method to achieve these goals, but they shared a growing assumption regarding their right to have a say. The New Woman, as she had been dubbed by the early twentieth century, defies easy definition, but one description does ring true: she was independent minded. Regardless of whether her path led to career or marriage or (for a still very small but growing number) both, the New Woman pushed against traditional boundaries and expected a greater degree of personal autonomy than previous generations of women. The New Woman was sometimes applauded but often derided, as some within society resisted the changes she represented. Becoming a New Woman required embracing the challenges of change, which was not always an easy choice to make. This proved true for Barbe. In the half decade after her successful YWCA involvement, she struggled to find a path away from her familiar deference toward a greater independence and New Womanhood.

Soon after the YWCA campaign, another reform opportunity offered Barbe a view of possible change when Juna's attention shifted to the ongoing battle to gain full female suffrage. The 1875 Supreme Court decision *Minor v. Happersett* had ruled that citizenship rights did not automatically confer voting rights, leading many female suffrage supporters, like Juna, to focus on state-level legislative efforts. This strategy did not always yield quick results, either. By the time Juna arrived in Illinois in 1894, women had gained only the limited right to vote in school board elections. Illinois activists had convinced legislators to support this by channeling attitudes about women's supposed natural nurturing instincts. Suffragists argued that this instinct rendered women more qualified to speak for matters affecting children and family. (In 1907 Barbe cast her first ballot in one of those school board elections, choosing a Lennon-endorsed family friend.) Illinois suffragists, however, viewed this 1891 win as only the first step. In 1909, after years of lobbying, state legislators were poised to vote on a proposed expansion of women's voting rights. Universal female suffrage represented both the greatest hope and the worst fear for many people, so this impending legislative decision inspired supporters and detractors to make their way to the capital. In an effort to showcase their popular strength, suffrage proponents commissioned a special train to travel the state and rally the troops. It left Chicago en route to Springfield, stopping along the way for speech making and to gather forces.

On April 14, 1909, this suffrage train arrived in Bloomington, and, despite a spike of tensions over the winter, Juna and Barbe stood together in this fight. They sang "America" with the throng of people crowded around the train before listening to dignitaries and suffrage activists that included Jane Addams and Illinois attorney Catherine Waugh McCullough. Addams's brief words were greeted with cheers, but, according to the local newspaper, McCullough really captured and held the people's attention with her powerful speech. After this short rally effort, the train moved on with Juna, Barbe, and two other local women aboard. Several more similarly enthusiastic stops followed before the suffrage train finally pulled into Springfield late that evening. The next morning brought the beginning of a full day of new experiences for Barbe. She and Juna joined the approximately five hundred suffragists and one hundred "antis" (as those who fought against female suffrage were popularly known) who converged on the statehouse. The women spent the morning urging their congressmen to vote for the suffrage bill before changing clothes to attend a luncheon at the Frank Lloyd Wright–designed home of local heiress and activist Susan Lawrence Dana. Dana devoted much of her time, influence, and considerable wealth to the fight for women's equality, and the luncheon attendees were charmed by both the hostess and her impressive home.

Their lobby efforts resumed that afternoon at a joint committee session where nineteen women and five men spoke on behalf of female suffrage. But speeches were not the only method used to show support. Suffragists all wore yellow daffodils, and the gallery was draped with a petition bearing fifteen thousand names demanding the right to vote. They seemed destined for success when the committee sent word that it was reporting favorably to the senate on the bill. The women returned in early May to lobby once again, but ultimately, despite their efforts and the favorable committee report, this voting rights bid would fail. To make the failure even more frustrating, Barbe also had to contend with a loss of pay for every school day missed lobbying for the vote because Bloomington teachers had no paid personal or vacation days. She also had to arrange for an acceptable substitute. Yet despite this failure, she deemed the effort a worthwhile experience. Like her prior YWCA campaign, her involvement in this exciting demand for political autonomy took her further down the path toward a sense of rightful independence. An organization called the American Women's League (AWL) strengthened that confidence even more.

The American Women's League, in some ways, epitomized the logical results of the popularity and evolution of women's organizations in the United States. During the mid-nineteenth century, separate (and largely racially segregated) women's groups had emerged as a way for women to bond outside the confines of their homes. These early groups primarily, although not exclusively, were social clubs centered on cultural and literary matters. By the late nineteenth century, these "clubs," so dubbed because of the word's historical association with male voluntary organizations, had become a central feature of society. Social and literary groups, like the Mosaic Circle or the A Volonte Club, still thrived, but now the club movement also encompassed large and well-organized reform associations attempting to solve pressing societal problems. The sheer potential of their numbers resulted in the creation of an umbrella organization, the General Federation of Women's Clubs, which in 1901 was granted a congressional charter. Groups like the WCTU and the National American Women's Suffrage Association could wield significant national political influence even without the vote. But smaller local organizations like the Bloomington Woman's Club could have immediate and important impacts in individual communities as well. The reform groups provided women without access to universal suffrage the power to effect change in the public sphere both locally and nationally while also providing (for some) another avenue for demanding voting rights.

Ironically, although it harnessed the popularity of the club movement, the AWL differed from most women's organizations in that its inception was the work of a man, not a woman. In 1902 magazine publisher and entrepreneur Edward Gardner Lewis relocated his publishing empire to newly purchased land near the 1904 St. Louis World's Fair site. Before long Lewis had been elected mayor of the newly incorporated town of University City, Missouri. The future looked bright until 1907, when the United States Postal Service raised the mailing rates for two of Lewis's most popular publications, the *Woman's Magazine* and the *Woman's Farm Journal*. Significant subscriber loss resulted. In December 1907, in an effort to rebuild his faltering publishing base, he established the American Woman's League. Women would form local AWL chapters, sell magazine subscriptions, and retain a portion of the sales fees to fund progressive reforms of their choosing. Response was quick and impressive. Within a year, seven hundred chapters existed across the country, including one in

Bloomington. By 1912 the organization would fail under the weight of constant financial problems, but despite those issues, as well as its quasi-capitalistic rather than purely philanthropic male founder, the local chapters initially offered avenues for female empowerment.

In early June 1909, an AWL representative contacted Juna, asking her to serve as a local booster for the organization. Juna agreed and invited other local women to attend an informational meeting. She also pushed a somewhat reluctant Barbe to come along. The meeting was a big success, and Barbe and Juna as well as numerous other women committed to the group. Despite the initial need for coercion, Barbe ultimately took a more active role in the local chapter. Juna turned down the request to serve as chair, but Barbe was elected secretary, and this position placed her in the center of the chapter's work (and struggles to survive) over the course of the next two years. At first things went well. Barbe helped to plan a successful magazine festival held in July. But despite its success, problems soon became apparent. First the group disagreed about how the subscription profits should be spent, and then a controversy arose when another chapter attempted to organize in the neighboring town of Normal. Barbe took center stage in both fights and was especially proactive in the latter. She wrote a letter to the AWL home office in St. Louis, exposing recruiting tactics she, and the other signers, deemed inappropriate. Apparently, local dramas like these were not anomalies. Concerns about the business affairs of the local chapters led the home office to implement plans to elect state regents as oversight officers. Throughout the fall and spring of 1909 and 1910, Barbe maintained a presence in the rented downtown office whenever possible and aggressively continued to try to gain subscriptions (including buying them for her relatives). She was rewarded for her efforts in May 1910, when the local chapter chose her as their state regent candidate. The final election was slated during the first-ever national AWL convention.

Thousands of women from all over the country converged on University City, Missouri, for this summer convention. Barbe and Juna traveled by train to St. Louis, joining other delegates from as far away as Connecticut already on board. Despite the regional differences, official photos taken at the convention offer visual confirmation of the actual lack of diversity typical of mainstream female Progressive Era activists. Invariably, these photos depict well-dressed white women donning elaborate hats. Lewis treated these middle-class female reformers to tours of the impressive beaux arts–inspired *Woman's Magazine* building, *Woman's National Daily* building, and Arts Academy building, before they spent the remainder of the day at University City's very popular Delmar Garden Amusement Park. They lunched at the park, and then afterward Edward Gardner Lewis gave an inspiring speech at the Delmar Garden's theater. The Missouri governor also spoke to the delegates, but after the ovation Lewis received the governor might have questioned the political wisdom of following the popular and charismatic man on his own turf. After dinner the women took part in the park amusements, courtesy of Lewis. Barbe was impressed by everything she saw, especially Lewis. And all seemed to agree that University City and the AWL were destined for success. They were wrong.

Barbe ultimately lost the state regent election to another Illinois delegate, but upon her return home she was reelected chapter secretary and continued to devote her precious spare time to staffing the office and recruiting members and subscriptions. She also spoke approvingly of the league's efforts in promoting causes such as suffrage and the kindergarten movement (still a novel idea that would not be implemented in Bloomington for another decade). Funds continued to be an issue, however, and the home office was not always forthcoming with subscription moneys owed to the local chapters. By early 1911, finances became so bad that all AWL members were assessed a fifty-cent fee. Half of this money was to go back into the local chapters, but the other half was to be loaned to Lewis's publishing business. This strategy failed to keep the Bloomington chapter afloat or save Lewis's publishing business. In May 1911, the Bloomington AWL had to give up its office space. In July Lewis Publishing went into receivership, much to Barbe's growing disgust with the group. The local chapter barely trudged on for the remainder of the year. In September fifteen women heard a "pitiful" letter from the state regent asking for funds to help Mr. Lewis weather his financial difficulties. Few were in favor of this aid, and by October the local chapter folded completely, followed in early 1912 by the demise of the national AWL. In the end, the AWL failed to deliver on its promises of philanthropic works or on its commitment to actual equal rights. Despite its failings, however, it did offer Barbe one of her first opportunities to take an active role not directly guided by Juna, and it fed her confidence.

Other developments during this time also reduced J. B. and Juna's impact on Barbe's daily life and provided a context for further independence. In late 1911, the Lennons threw themselves into another evangelical revival that for months drew them away from the house. Barbe complained more emphatically, albeit still privately, about their involvement in what she considered a ridiculous time waste. "Hope it won't drive Mrs L to the verge of insanity like the [Billy] Sunday meetings did. Never think about those times that it doesn't give me a shudder."[1] Then in May 1912, Juna was elected the Woman's Club's vice president, and she spent much of the next year actively involved in the prestigious club's philanthropic efforts to build playgrounds, clean up alleys, establish garbage guidelines, implement food inspections, and launch a "welfare campaign" to aid poor women and children by helping to fund a new day nursery (an early version of child day care). During this same period, J. B. aggressively lobbied Congress to establish a US Commission on Industrial Relations tasked with investigating national working conditions. Once this commission gained approval, J. B. received a presidential appointment as one of its inaugural commissioners. Over the next few years, J. B. traveled extensively, as he conducted field research throughout the nation and attended frequent meetings in Washington, DC. When available, Juna accompanied him on his trips as well. In the midst of this venture, J. B. also won reelection as the general secretary of the JTU after losing it in 1909, largely as a result of his very unpopular temperance stance. So by 1912, changes were under way. The Lennons were less of a daily fixture in Barbe's life, her self-confidence was growing—albeit slowly—and the death of the AWL left space for new interests. This space would be filled by a variety of pursuits over the next few years, but in the immediate aftermath of the AWL's demise she turned to the national issue occupying many people's minds, the 1912 election.

The year 1912 brought a contentious presidential election with four rival candidates: incumbent Republican William Howard Taft, "Bull Moose" Progressive Teddy Roosevelt, (progressive-leaning) Democrat Woodrow Wilson, and Socialist Eugene Debs. Barbe's life with the Lennons meant that she was well versed in the political and labor topics of the time, but, typical of her past deference, her opinions on these matters tended to simply echo theirs. This election offered a chance to demonstrate that although she remained influenced by the Lennons' endeavors, she also was capable of independent thought. During the primary season, both Wilson and Roosevelt made stops in Bloomington to personally lobby for votes, and John Harlan (son of the former Supreme Court justice) stopped in town to speak on behalf of President Taft. Once the general election campaign got under way, William Jennings Bryan and Senator James Beauchamp "Champ" Clark campaigned in Bloomington for Wilson. Jane Addams and Bloomington native Illinois Progressive Party gubernatorial candidate Frank Funk toured the state in support of Roosevelt. Ultimately, Woodrow Wilson won the national vote for the presidency, but Illinois proved to be divided. The Progressive Roosevelt carried the state by a large margin for president, but the Democratic candidate won the governorship.

Like Illinois, J. B.'s loyalties also must have been torn. Illinois Progressives had approached him as a possible candidate for Congress in 1912 on the Progressive Party ticket, and the party's platform included things he had long supported: women's equal suffrage, minimum wages for women, child labor laws, and worker's compensation laws. But his AFL mentor and boss Samuel Gompers was a staunch supporter of Wilson, who he believed to be the best bet for big labor. J. B.'s contrary stance on the temperance issue illustrated he was not afraid to defy the AFL party line, but he needed the support of both the president and Gompers if he was to receive the appointment to the industrial commission that he so desired. So although he spoke in favor of some state-level Progressive candidates, he supported the Democratic ticket. (Their support would be rewarded after Wilson's win with unprecedented presidential backing for the AFL and J. B.'s appointment to the industrial commission.) Barbe also attended

Democratic and Progressive Party meetings and stump speeches, but defying her usual family allegiance she declared her support for the Bull Moose Party. Illinois women still did not have the right to vote for the president, but she did cast her ballot for the Progressive Party's female candidate for University of Illinois trustee. Throughout the campaign season, she also attended most of the events with friends rather than the Lennons. This growing pattern of personal autonomy increasingly was becoming the norm.

Other interests also enhanced her potential ability to claim further independence during this time. Society accepted, and by this point actively encouraged, a woman's role as a consumer. According to male-female norms, women spent money, but men managed it. Despite the assumption that finance was a masculine endeavor, in reality as an unmarried adult woman Barbe's income was solely in her legal control. Plus, from her earliest working days, she had displayed an interest in managing her own finances. She sometimes splurged on clothes—she loved to shop—but other than those occasional sprees, she proved to be very frugal. She also had the advantage of living with the Lennons. Her thriftiness combined with this rent-free status meant that despite her low wages, her savings had steadily grown. By 1909 her confidence in both the market and her abilities had led her to complement this base with more aggressive strategies. She made personal loans (with interest charged) to friends and her siblings and purchased certificates, bonds, and insurance. By 1912 she also held small mortgage notes on several homes in Bloomington. In January 1914, she combined these strategies by lending eight hundred dollars to a local businessman in exchange for stock in the local Pantagraph Printing and Stationery Company. She proved adept at building a financial safety net.

Her desire for financial control and stability likely can be attributed, at least in part, to her family history. Resources on the Egger family farm had been strained, and her father had provided no monetary support after sending her to Bloomington. In reality, he likely had expected her to contribute to the family coffer after she began teaching. Despite knowing her parents sometimes struggled, Barbe apparently disagreed. Even when her father faced eviction from the family farm, she offered no financial help. Her father seems to be at the center of this decision. She loaned money to her siblings. And even though her brother failed to repay her in a timely fashion, she ultimately loaned him (and her other siblings) money again as the years passed. She also gave money to her mother (in the years after her father died). Clearly, she did not object to mixing family and money. But in this case, she simply blamed her father's stubbornness, and although she was sorry that her mother was being forced to move from her home, she did not step in. Perhaps "punishing" her father was a way to achieve a sense of vindication for a childhood she remembered as harsh and unloving. This dynamic affected more than just her approach to finances. Throughout her father's life, she remained concerned for her mother's happiness and health, but when faced with a choice between her role as the Eggers' daughter and her role as the Lennons' surrogate daughter, she consistently chose the latter. She sometimes struggled with guilt over this choice, particularly where her mother was concerned, but Barbe clearly had transferred her sense of family allegiance to the Lennons. And despite the ongoing friction between Barbe and Juna, this choice offered the security needed to continue her sporadic steps toward greater independence.

Her teaching career had benefited from this newfound assurance as well. For example, in 1912 the superintendent sang her praises to another administrator, and in 1913 he transferred her to the more challenging sixth grade class of the Edwards School because of her proven abilities. Regardless of this professional growth, whether Barbe saw teaching in Bloomington as her future is unclear. Her actions indicate a sense of restlessness. In January 1912, she took an art class at Illinois Wesleyan University in Bloomington, and this pastime soon became a passion. She continued to watch every penny, but she never balked at paying tuition or buying paints and ceramic supplies. In early 1913, she added music lessons to her schedule and eventually even purchased her own piano after Juna sold the family's piano. (Tensions between the two had lessened but not disappeared, and Barbe was devastated by the sale, which she felt was a personal punishment.) In contrast to these artistic endeavors, she also successfully completed a "Chicago Correspondence School" course in stenography and typewriting. Female office workers were on the rise, so perhaps she initially envisioned a new career path before realizing (much like in teaching) that as office support positions transitioned from traditionally male clerks to female secretaries, opportunities for advancement disappeared and paychecks diminished. She also briefly considered staking a claim in a western mining community, but her brother's lack of success in that arena quickly dampened her interest. Even within her own profession, she displayed restlessness. In 1913 and early 1914, she investigated teaching positions in Montana and the Dakotas, and in the autumn of 1914 she seriously considered a teaching supervisor job in Singapore. All of these musings reflect a lack of certainty on her part. Even with historical hindsight, it is difficult to assess whether she was trying to mold herself into better marriage material, advance her career, or simply pass time.

By 1914 Barbe's growing autonomy showed in other ways as well. In March 1914 she proudly declared, "[I] stayed alone last four nights—did not mind a bit." In the past, when the Lennons traveled either someone stayed with Barbe or she slept at a friend's or a neighbor's, as leaving her alone worried the Lennons. J. B. even suggested that Barbe might want to find a temporary boarding situation to alleviate her isolation during the Lennons' frequent trips. He had not suggested a permanent move, but the comment hurt and angered Barbe. She defiantly declared, "If I ever go I'll never come back to this house." She continued to simmer with anger about the perceived rejection and several weeks later returned to the subject again. "[I have] half a notion to leave here and board." Barbe was more than thirty years old, so both her petulant attitude and the Lennons' apprehension seem slightly overdone; nonetheless, their dynamic of nearly fifteen years offers some insight. The Lennons clearly thought of Barbe as family, so she likely had no real reason to worry about permanent eviction. But Juna did tend to hint at that threat when angered, so Barbe's uncertainty was not completely unwarranted. At the same time, the Lennons' desire for continued oversight during their frequent absences may have reflected concern for both Barbe and themselves. Perhaps expecting a certain level of "daughterly" care as they grew older, they may have viewed her growing independence with concern. If she left, then they would be left alone. Or perhaps they genuinely worried about her safety or actions when she stayed home alone. Regardless of their reasons, Barbe continued to live in their home, but as 1914 turned to 1915 her autonomous steps continued as well.[2]

This growing independence reflected both old interests and new. She joined the recently organized "Ladies Local Option" (temperance) group, was reelected president of the A Volonte Club, attended a lecture on "sex hygiene" that promoted sex education for young people, and took tango lessons. She also pursued a longtime interest in the Unitarian Church. In the past, she had avoided the Unitarian because she believed it angered Juna. But for Barbe, the local Unitarian motto of "the church of the open door and the open mind" spoke to her desire for connection and security, while it also appealed to her sense of progressive mindedness. When the Lennons' prolonged absences in 1914 provided opportunity for freer attendance, she took advantage, and in early November she, along with three girlfriends, officially joined. This step marked the beginning of a lifelong commitment to a church that devalued dogma and valued tolerance, equality, and respect for others. Its influence would help shape her future, but in the immediate period it brought "Mr. E." into her life. Otto Erdmann was a piano tuner by trade and Barbe's new Sunday-school teacher. One week after they met, he and another male friend walked Barbe and two of her girlfriends home. According to Barbe, giggles were the defining feature of this first walk, but it also seemed to offer a serious diversion as she pondered her future.

In early November 1914, her actions pointed toward several different potential paths. She was considering investing twelve hundred dollars in a beauty parlor, but she also was investigating a job opportunity as a supervisor of a grammar school in Singapore. The latter seemed to indicate a desire to seek a path away from Bloomington, but joining the Unitarian church and investing in a local business would solidify autonomous roots in Bloomington. In the past, the Lennons' guidance would have held full sway in this decision-making process, but she had become less reliant on their views. J. B. had quickly declared that he considered her potential ownership in a beauty parlor business as disgraceful and beneath her. But she did not immediately negate the idea. She also consciously rejected the Lennons' views on the Unitarian Church membership. Now Erdmann had entered the picture, and this time Juna quickly registered her disapproval. Contrary to Barbe's past habit of deferring the ultimate authority for her decisions to the Lennons, she did not immediately replace their judgment for her own. She did, however, seek some direction.

Not long after meeting Erdmann, Barbe consulted a local psychic, Mrs. Schultz, to have her "cards read." This visit was not her first. Over the years, she had eagerly and frequently sought out supernatural venues. She claimed disbelief in such things, but she and her friends often participated in so-called supernatural activities such as séances, table "tipping," automatic writing, and Ouija-board messaging. They also pursued future forecasts from clairvoyants, palmists, and card readers. Not entirely surprisingly, Mrs. Schultz's cards predicted marriage for Barbe within the next year. This marriage prognostication also was not Barbe's first. In November 1910, Mrs. Schultz had predicted a wedding within eighteen months, and in 1907 a different clairvoyant had declared 1908 the year she would marry. Perhaps because of this repetition, Barbe did not focus on the marriage forecast. Instead, she voiced frustration that Mrs. Schultz's projections offered no direction regarding whether she should pursue the supervisory position in Singapore. Without clear answers from the cards, she came to her own conclusions, and her decisions reflected both continuity and change. When it came to the beauty salon purchase, she did bow to J. B.'s disapproval and passed on the investment. But she retained her Unitarian membership, and most defiantly she continued her relationship with Erdmann, despite Juna's vocal disapproval. As for the Singapore opportunity, she may well have chosen to forego this opportunity because of her budding romance with Erdmann.

After several shared walks home and Sunday-school meetings, Barbe (perhaps inspired by Mrs. Schultz's prognostications) finally asked Erdmann to join the family for dinner after church. This visit signaled a shift in their relationship, and it was followed by three more visits in five days. At the conclusion of the third, he took things to the next level by asking Juna (as J. B. was out of town) if he could "call" on Barbe. Juna agreed but not without reservations, and less than a week later she complained to Barbe that she "did not run a boarding house and didn't care to have him to meals three times a week." She also demanded that Barbe gather further information regarding Erdmann's "character" from the Unitarian minister and warned that if Barbe didn't, then she would. Juna then directed her ire at Erdmann and "discouraged" him from calling. Her efforts failed to stop the developing relationship, and when J. B. returned home the next week for the Christmas holiday his apparent approval overrode Juna's disapproval.[3]

Over the next few weeks, the couple saw each other several times a week. In line with traditional "calling," he came to the house, where they would visit with supervision near. They also socialized with other people their own age—unchaperoned but in groups—reminiscent of her Hopedale years. Indicative of changing times, however, the two also went on the occasional "date." Dating, previously a slang term used only by the working class, had become an acceptable, albeit novel, term to describe new and increasingly common courting behavior. Dating reflected changes in social interaction, as urbanization and technological advances created new spaces and places for socializing. Shifts in ideas about acceptable male-female interaction also played a role in the changing dynamic. "Dating" was different from "calling" on several fronts. A woman asked a man to call on her at home, which normally necessitated family approval and provided the woman and her parents (or surrogates) greater control. Contrary to that dynamic, dating often meant attending an event or visiting a public venue, necessitating a purchase of some sort, such as buying tickets to the movies or a sporting event or an amusement park or treating a date to an ice cream or a soda or dinner. Society assumed male control of money, which led to a reversal of prior norms. If the man paid, then the man needed to do the asking; thus, significant control for the courting ritual transferred into his hands. By the 1920s, dating would be the norm, but Erdmann and Barbe's relationship occurred during the overlapping of old and new.

At first the two seemed to be negotiating the fluctuating norms well. Erdmann played cards or had popcorn at her house under the watchful eye of Juna, but Barbe also attended basketball games and movies with him. As January unfolded, their growing admiration seemed to be mutual. She took him to meet some close friends in Hopedale, and he asked for Barbe's picture, a classic Victorian courting ritual. She complemented his Sunday-school leadership, and he told her she looked pretty in her red hat, white coat, and muff, an ensemble that she put considerable thought into. Regardless of their apparently developing feelings, however, their relationship remained a platonic one. For Erdmann, the lack of privacy proved to be the primary barrier. They almost always were either in the eye of the "public" or under the watchful gaze of Juna. Barbe had no experience at being part of a couple. And unfortunately, she would have little time to come to terms with the potential emotional or physical elements of this status. Once the holidays were over, Juna joined J. B. in Washington, and with that buffer removed the relationship shifted.

Two months after the couple's first giggle-filled walk, two days after Juna's departure, and one day after Erdmann's flattering words about her pretty red ensemble, Barbe noted two firsts in her journal: Erdmann called her "Barbara" rather than Miss Egger (as Victorian etiquette mandated), and he tried to "be affectionate." She rebuffed his attempts, but after he returned from a weeklong trip he again became "very affectionate." She again pushed him away, but he insisted that "surely it wasn't wrong . . . when two people liked each other." As she described it, he then "kissed me about 20 times. . . . Wouldn't let me go until I kissed him." The next day, they visited for an hour before he once again was "very affectionate [and] tried to make me set on his knee but [I] wouldn't." She faithfully documented what happened, but she never clearly elaborated how she felt. She had no experience with intimacy of this kind, and her hesitancy indicates she was uncomfortable with it, but she also struggled to sort out her feelings. Like courtship rituals, ideas about acceptable levels of physical contact were in flux as well. By the 1920s, a kiss would no longer mean a couple had to consider themselves engaged, and premarital intimacy (short of actual intercourse) would no longer be vilified by all. But again their relationship occurred within the context of the overlap of old and new. In much the same way, her feelings must have collided with expectations. She needed time to sort out the resulting collision, but time was not in the cards.[4]

The day after she rebuffed his latest efforts at "affection," his attitude seemed chilly, and Juna's return home the next day increased this coolness. Acting on either instinct or rumor, she immediately stormed over to the neighbor's (Viola Reed) and demanded that Reed reveal Barbe's whereabouts and whether she was still seeing "that man." Viola Reed attempted to assure her that Barbe had done nothing wrong. Barbe had kept the Reeds apprised of her comings and goings and even was in bed before them. How much credit Juna gave this statement is unclear, especially given the fact that Reed's loyalty seemed to lay with Barbe. She told Barbe that she was not "in sympathy with Mrs L's narrow ways" and was on her "side."[5] Juna's reactions may have reflected concerns about Erdmann personally, but they also were grounded in proper Victorian-era etiquette regarding courtship. Reed's characterization of Juna as "narrow" illustrates changing Progressive Era ideas about "dating" that even a respectable married woman could accept, although it is unclear whether she knew of Erdmann's eagerness to move even further beyond those emerging norms. Barbe seemed to be stuck between the two ways of thinking. She had come to appreciate her growing independence, but her feelings for Erdmann left her yearning for a time when their engagement would have been assumed. Plus, despite her friction with Juna, she also still longed for her approval and not just because she believed Erdmann's chilly attitude was going to be difficult to thaw without it. Over the next few months, Barbe's efforts to save their relationship consumed her thoughts, and she held on to possibility far longer than hindsight indicates was reasonable.

From the day Juna returned home, things changed between the erstwhile couple. They saw each other much less frequently, and he even stopped sitting with her at church. Plus, he began to offer a string of excuses for his unavailability: he had a headache; he had to write; he was tired; he was going out of town for work. Sometimes he would make a promise and simply fail to follow through. Barbe responded to this retreat with confusion: "[I] don't know why he acts so, perhaps it's my imagination."[6] But she also resorted to investigation. She went by his boardinghouse nearly every day for weeks to see if his mailbox was full, knowing that if it was empty, then he must be in town to pick it up. Finally, after a month of confusion, she maneuvered an after-church walk, and he was forced to talk. Unfortunately, Barbe was not pleased with the result. He offered a variety of explanations for why they had to stop seeing each other. He told her that he enjoyed their visits, but she was too serious. He planned to never marry, as he wanted the freedom to date different girls, especially if he knew a girl was lonely and needed company. Plus, given his resistance to a long-term commitment, he felt it would not be right to continue to see her. They were both too old to prolong a relationship with no marriage in the future. Barbe tried to assuage his worries and averred that she was neither serious nor thinking of marriage, but to no avail. He rebuffed her assertions, and their talk left her depressed. That evening she visited Mrs. Schultz again, but this time her career was not her focus. The psychic declared that Barbe was not the problem; instead, Erdmann was put off by someone else in the house, which Barbe assumed to be Juna. Mrs. Schultz assured her that despite this issue, he would come back and they would marry. Despite her prior claims of supernatural disbelief, she took this prognostication to heart. Against all apparent reason, Barbe continued to hope.

The next seven weeks were marked by the same dynamic as the previous month. Barbe continued to seek out contact, and Erdmann continued to distance himself. Two weeks after their "talk," Viola Reed offered classic "play hard to get" advice—"Just let him alone and he'll come back"—which prompted Barbe's first clear declaration of love: "I hope so as I dearly love him and enjoy him so much." Another two weeks passed, and their distant and formal communication left Barbe heartbroken. "[I] have thought so much of him the last few days that my head fairly bursts." She continued to pursue interaction, and any communication at all bred hope. The Lennons clearly had to notice that Erdmann no longer called, but it is unknown whether they were aware of her deep despair. They did, however, realize something was amiss, and Barbe's versions of their attempts at communication echo past interactions. In early April, J. B. tried to reach out. "Kid what's the matter with you the last two months. You seem so restless. Was amazed when I came home and found you so." She appreciated his concern but deflected it with claims of overwork. Two weeks later, Juna's queries and her response took an entirely different tone. Juna demanded to know why Barbe had been moping about the house since November and warned her that if she did not snap out of it, they would need to hire help and take her room. So from Barbe's view, J. B. cared (even if she would not share her feelings with him), and Juna once again threatened banishment. Clearly, everyone in the Lennon home was unhappy with Barbe's attitude, but no one was sure how to change it, including Barbe, who stubbornly clung to her hope for a positive outcome.[7]

Two days after Juna's "threat," Barbe arranged another talk with Erdmann. She was in a "nervous tremor" as she asked him if she had done something to offend him that would explain his changed behavior. He again explained that it was nothing she had done. He simply could not continue to call on her and have people talk of their impending marriage when that was an impossibility. But "he hoped we'd always be friends." Either from a desire to prolong the conversation or taking his promise of friendship to heart, she asked for his advice. She shared details about possible job opportunities, her home life, and specifically her complaints about Juna. His advice was succinct: "[He] told me to leave . . . and that I was too dependent on others . . . and [should] want to teach out of town." Even though she, in fact, had recently considered leaving Bloomington, she hesitated to agree that moving was necessary for greater independence. Their conversation ended on that dissonance, and they shook hands and parted ways. He, no doubt, felt that this conversation finally made his feelings clear, but Barbe's closing remark that she "valued his friendship more than any other man" spoke to a different conclusion.[8]

Over the next two weeks, her continued hope is evidenced, as she noted every sighting and mailbox status. Reality finally quashed her fantasies when she found out, despite his declaration that he would never marry, that Erdmann and a local cashier had wed. She was devastated. She tried to find some sort of solace in the fact that the couple's relationship was so new (no more than six weeks, by her estimate) that their Unitarian minister had assumed Barbe was to be the bride. Initial rumors around town also named Barbe as the likely bride, much to Juna's annoyance. Barbe spent a short period wallowing in deep self-pity, and then she never mentioned Otto Erdmann again. That is not to say that the short-lived relationship and its unfortunate end left her unaffected. In many ways, it was the final catalyst inspiring big change. Barbe had been moving steadily toward something over the past few years, but it had been unclear what that something should be. The decision was now made. She was over thirty, and her chance at love and marriage had apparently passed. She was now free to concentrate on becoming an independent-minded, career New Woman. To improve that path, however, she needed to make a change. But rather than leaving to find that path, she took advantage of opportunities within reach. One month after she learned of Erdmann's wedding, she enrolled at Illinois State Normal University (ISNU) for the summer session.

4

New Woman, 1915–1918

Barbe's entry into Illinois State Normal University took her further down the path toward the educated, independent, and career-minded New Woman she aspired to be. She also was not alone when she looked to higher education as a road to change. Although still representing only a tiny percentage of the total population, college attendance increased more than 50 percent for each of the two decades before World War I. Women's attendance rose even faster. In part this rise could be attributed to increased access as the number of public universities grew, but Progressive Era ideas about education also played a role. Progressive reforms had led to more high schools, an increased emphasis on courses identified as practical (industrial arts and domestic science), and more stringent requirements for teachers. In response and in conjunction with these changing ideas, many schools of higher education and teacher training facilities also altered their long-established programs of study, including Illinois State Normal University. Barbe's enrollment at ISNU occurred during the midst of its efforts to implement many of these progressive ideas about education.

Throughout the nineteenth century, ISNU had served primarily as a "normal," that is, teacher training, school as well as a venue for students to gain preparatory education for entry into four-year colleges. In the early twentieth century, however, ISNU undertook the challenge of the changing times and in 1907 (fifty years after its founding) took advantage of a new Illinois law to add a "Teacher's College" that offered a four-year bachelor's degree in education. The institution retained its Normal School but also introduced manual arts (1908) and domestic science (1909) sequences to its options as reaction to the shifting needs of the practical education movement. Planners anticipated men's enrollment in the four-year Teacher's College degree program in order to qualify for the growing number of professional positions as high school teachers and administrators, while the two-year "Normal School" diploma would continue to prepare women for elementary and specialized subject teaching. ISNU president David Felmley summed up the reasoning behind this strategy in a 1914 speech to the National Education Association (NEA): "Most of your teachers are young women who will not remain in the workforce longer than five years. . . . Two years is as long a period of special training as we may justly require."[1]

Women continued to enter the Normal School, and they flocked to the domestic science option, but, despite Felmley's assumptions, women also entered the Teacher's College. In fact, in 1916 and 1917, women slightly outnumbered men as graduating seniors. Both factors, no doubt, served as the impetus to add a four-year home economics program in 1918. As a whole, the curricular changes did help to attract both men and women to ISNU. More than 2,800 students attended ISNU in 1914–1915, as compared to the historic low of 387 in 1903–1904. New teacher certification laws played a role in this growth as well. In 1914 Illinois implemented progressive-minded reforms designed to put trained professionals into the classroom. Prospective new Illinois teachers now faced more stringent rules than in prior years. One option for certification required teachers to show proof of graduation from a certified high school and earn a passing score on an eighteen-subject qualifying exam. Another allowed them to avoid this exam but only if they had graduated from a normal (teacher prep) school and showed proof of a minimum of one year successful practice (student) teaching. As an established educator, Barbe could renew her teaching certificate by showing proof of successful continued employment and continuing education via regularly offered Teachers' Institutes. Yet she chose to join the growing numbers of working educators, hopeful teachers, and future administrators taking advantage of ISNU's recently evolved curriculum. Her choice reflected the expanded opportunities made possible by progressive reform, but her experience was also shaped by the lingering gender bias inherent in Felmley's statement.

Barbe began her college career with two summer courses, Domestic Science and Teaching Process. The latter focused on the process and theory of pedagogy, whereas the Domestic Science course centered on the scientific, economic, and sociological aspects of kitchen management as well as a pragmatic approach to cooking. By 1915 domestic science and home economics programs had grown in popularity, but not without dissent. Many contemporary feminists condemned these fields of study as part of a strategy to funnel female students into "appropriate" courses designed only to prepare women as future wives. Numerous eastern women's colleges staunchly refused to incorporate home economics programs. They argued the programs lacked intellectual vigor and reinforced traditional gender roles. Both charges were contrary to the intent of home economics' turn-of-the-century founders, in particular Ellen Richards. Richards was the first woman to graduate from the Massachusetts Institute of Technology, and she envisioned home economics (or euthenics, as she preferred) as a path to professional fields where educated women applied scientific techniques to nutrition, sanitation, and home management.

The programs did play a role in the growing commonality of gender divisions in education that tied women more closely to domestic identities. But they provided opportunities for intellectual and professional empowerment as well. The subject matter may have been cooking, sewing, and home management, but the method incorporated business, economics, sociology, and science. This approach complied with the central Progressive Era themes of scientific management, social housekeeping, and professionalism, while also preparing women for various social reform careers. Plus, in a time when opportunities for women's advancement in education had begun to narrow, the degrees led to emerging and still viable avenues of employment as specialized subject teachers or supervisors. In addition, the growing prevalence of domestic science and home economic baccalaureate degrees became one of the few roads women could take to faculty positions in the overwhelmingly male-dominated world of higher education.

Barbe clearly viewed her domestic science program as a path for intellectual and career growth, not as a housewife preparatory sequence, but her busy schedule left little time to ponder the broader implications of her field of study. For just over eight weeks, she attended full days of classes before adjourning to the library almost every night to study late into the evening. She responded to this rigor with enthusiasm and pride. High marks and compliments from her professors on individual assignments elicited joy, as did her final course grades. She earned a 94 percent in Domestic Science and a 90 percent in Teaching Process. Considerable time was devoted to achieving these high marks, but she still carved out space to meet her new school friends for lunches, dinners, shopping, and university or community events. In years past, summer commonly brought travel with the Lennons and hurt feelings if an invitation was not forthcoming. So a late-summer decision was telling of her expanded sense of independence. With no drama, she voluntarily declined Juna's invitation to accompany the couple to Chicago. She simply decided that she did not want to go. Instead, she took a four-week solo trip west for a visit with a former Hopedale teaching colleague. This autonomy and her sense of confidence expanded and contracted over the next few years, as continuity and change continued to vie for supremacy, but in hindsight this summer session at ISNU marked a defining and expansive shift, from which she never completely deflated.

In September 1915, Bloomington's school year and Barbe's teaching responsibilities recommenced, and her time at ISNU temporarily ended. Nonetheless, not all remnants of her growing autonomy dissipated. J. B.'s work with the US Commission on Industrial Relations kept him (and Juna) away from home sporadically that fall and almost continuously from January until May 1916. J. B. clearly had come to accept Barbe's growing independence. He even relied on her to take care of the house and bills. Juna, however, had not completely given up her effort to manage Barbe's life. For example, in March 1916, she tried and failed to convince Barbe to come east and stay with them instead of returning to the classroom for the spring session. Juna's request had been prompted by worries regarding Barbe's health, concerns that may have held some validity. Beginning in the fall of 1915 and continuing into the spring, some unnamed ailment led her doctor to once again prescribe calomel. Her prior calomel use had been linked with stress, but physicians prescribed it for a variety of reasons during this era. Nevertheless, with current-day knowledge of the debilitating properties of the mercury-based "medicine," it is not surprising that she became even sicker. In March 1916, her face swelled almost beyond recognition, and she felt horrible for several weeks. Eventually, a different doctor decided that the swelling was caused by either her malfunctioning liver or her kidney. He took her off the calomel and put her on a soft diet, and the swelling diminished. These periodic health setbacks notwithstanding, all other indications show she continued to thrive during the Lennons' absences.

An attitude of openness to new experiences characterizes her approach to life during this period. She enjoyed her usual pastimes, but widening interests also emerged. The Unitarian Church remained central to her life. She joined the Women's Alliance (a Unitarian women's group devoted to education and advocacy for women's issues), became a Sunday-school teacher, and led a girls' church group organized to study nature. She remained active with the A Volonte Club but also joined a hiking club made up of local enthusiasts, both male and female. This group met on weekends for daylong hikes in the countryside that typically culminated in late-afternoon cold picnics on warm days and outdoor fires on cool ones. Additional free time was spent on the always favorite shopping as well as feeding her cultural and intellectual needs with theater, movies, and lectures. She continued teaching her sixth grade classes at Edwards, but she also began to display more interest in the intellectual and social forces outside the classroom that shaped her experience. Over the course of the year, she attended a variety of lectures connected to educational topics. Some of these lectures focused on theoretical and academic ideas regarding approaches to teaching, such as the "pedagogy of preadolescence period" and the "advancement of the child." Others provided anecdotal reports on the practical applications of introducing progressive changes into the schools such as "gym" or playgrounds. Other speakers shed light on the struggles faced by teachers attempting to bring reforms to the working environment of the teaching profession itself.

In January 1916, Barbe heard the plight of one of those reformers when a teacher from the Chicago Federation of Teachers (CFT) delivered a spirited description of their decadelong fight for survival. In 1902 the female grade school teachers of Chicago had decided to affiliate their teachers federation with the AFL's Chicago Federation of Labor. Unfortunately, many people viewed the women's association with an industrial labor union as unseemly behavior for a teacher. In 1905 the Chicago Board of Education officially condemned the connection as intolerable. They subsequently tried to break the union by implementing "yellow-dog contracts" that denied teachers the right to union affiliation, thus escalating a long battle for the union's survival. Unfortunately, soon after Barbe's attendance at the CFT talk, the teachers lost this fight when the Illinois Supreme Court ruled that school boards could deny teachers the right to organize. Nevertheless, their grassroots fight for "bread-and-butter" issues such as salaries, pensions, and tenure had by this point resulted in the birth of the national union—the American Federation of Teachers (AFT).

Barbe was clearly interested in their plight, and she was well versed in union solidarity. She had been privy to J. B.'s day-to-day work as a labor activist and had attended the JTU and AFL annual conventions on a regular basis, often sitting in the gallery, listening to the debates and business. Nonetheless, as part of this ongoing socialization, she had also been steeped in the AFL leaders' traditional ideas about women that emphasized a woman's place in the home and a man's place in the workforce. This attitude had resulted in a largely male-focused conservative union movement. As the Chicago fight illustrated, society in general also had strong views about teachers and unions. So despite her interest in their struggle, her prior immersion in the world of union activism, and her emerging independence during this time span, she demonstrated no commitment to the idea that a union was necessary to achieve her career goals. Instead, she remained determined to continue her college education. Toward that goal, she once again excitedly registered for the summer session at

ISNU. It had been a year since she had taken a class, and she was eager to join the three thousand other enrollees registered for that summer, but unfortunately her home life thwarted the plan.

After a long absence, the Lennons had arrived back in Bloomington in early May 1916. Their homecoming immediately affected Barbe's day-to-day life. She felt compelled to arrange her schedule around them to a greater degree, and complaints about "Mrs L" signaled the resumption of the role of "daughter." Plus, Juna had big summer plans of her own that did not coincide with Barbe's. The house was getting an indoor flush toilet, electrical wiring, and new hardwood floors. As the plethora of advertisements attested, technological modernization and home beautification were important facets of middle-class efforts to separate themselves from the growing industrial working class. J. B. may have worked with the laboring classes, but Juna in particular was sensitive to appearances. Everything from furniture, rugs, and electric vacuums to radiator heating, new plumbing, and electric lights were touted as the new must-haves for middle-class homes, and Juna was determined to have them all. After consults with a variety of contractors, she set this considerable project in motion. Construction itself was in the hands of workmen, but the inconvenience and extra work surrounding these updates fell largely to Barbe.

Barbe's independence had grown, but Juna could still insert influence sufficient to sway her path, and Barbe knew that she could not manage a full class schedule and Juna's expectations at home. As a result, although she hated to do it, Barbe decided to hold off on school. So instead of matriculating, she spent the summer cleaning and organizing the house according to Juna's wishes. Nonetheless, during her limited free time, she continued to turn to friends rather than to the Lennons. A girlfriend even decided that sufficient time had passed since the Otto Erdmann debacle for Barbe to consider other men. She introduced Barbe to a visiting bachelor friend, a "Mr. Freid" from Chicago. As a result of this setup, the two had several dates where they went to the movies, shared chocolate shakes, and took pictures with Barbe's newly purchased Kodak camera (a replacement for the first mass-marketed camera, her much-loved "little Brownie"). Unlike her prior relationship with Erdmann, their summer conversations stayed away from the personal and squarely on the communal. They discussed the escalating European war, the growing threat of German submarines, and the emerging eastern epidemic of "infantile paralysis" (polio). Nothing came of their brief friendship, but as the fall approached Barbe quietly reached a decision about her future: she would return to college regardless of Juna's perceived or real needs.

In order to reach this educational goal, Barbe took a surprising step: she took a leave of absence from teaching. ISNU promised book costs would not exceed fifteen dollars per year and waived tuition for any present or future Illinois teacher, so with her savings and rent-free home she could afford to take an unpaid leave. For much of her life, this step would have seemed somewhat uncharacteristic, but given her growing independence of late the choice is less surprising. Nonetheless, perhaps fearing attempts to change her mind, she apparently discussed this plan with no one—not the Lennons, friends, or any colleagues—until after she had made the decision. Once she decided, however, she did need permission to take the leave. She contacted her superintendent, and he enthusiastically endorsed the idea. He even helped her draft a letter requesting the leave of absence. The Bloomington School Board quickly approved, and it was official. Her excitement over this next step is clear in her September 1916 journal entry: "First Day of Illinois State Normal University!"[2] True, she had attended classes the prior summer, but her new status as a full-time student during the regular term certainly qualified this as a symbolic "first day." And on that joyful note, she joined the rather elite cultural cohort of college women.

They were not the first generation of women to attend college, but they did bring a new attitude. The educational pioneers of the 1870s and 1880s had been responsible for demonstrating to naysayers that women not only had the right to higher education but the ability to succeed. As such they had to prove their intellectual capacity as well as their physical and emotional endurance. By 1910 the New Woman third-generation college attendee assumed her right to a place (even if others did not), and she wanted a complete and well-rounded experience. She worked hard, but she also believed in the importance of play. Barbe continued to live in the Lennons' Bloomington home rather than in approved student housing nearer to the Normal campus, but she did her best to embrace college life as defined by this third generation of college women. She made new friends, was invited to join the coed Wrightonian Society (a literary and debating club dating back to 1857), attended social events and games, and earned good grades in her classes, which included Sewing, Geography, Psychology, Gymnastics, and Rhetoric. College consumed much of her life, but even her intense focus could not block out the world-changing topics on most people's minds: war, peace, and their connection to the coming presidential election.

The US constitutional amendment granting women universal suffrage was still four years in the future, but Illinois women finally had won their state fight in 1913 and gained the right to vote in presidential elections. Not surprisingly, suffrage supporter Juna threw herself into Democratic politics during the 1916 lead-up to her first presidential vote. She and J. B. actively campaigned for President Woodrow Wilson's reelection as well as other Democratic candidates. Like Juna, Barbe had also staunchly supported women's fight for the vote, but, somewhat surprisingly, Barbe seemed somewhat apathetic about the election itself and cynical about the Lennons' wholesale involvement. She complained that Juna seemed to have had lost her head and condemned J. B.'s support for Wilson as merely a ploy to obtain a political appointment. But even setting aside this latter possibility, their support made sense. Wilson was the more progressive of the candidates, and he had shown himself to be friendlier to labor unions (especially the AFL) than any past president. Plus, Barbe's comments undoubtedly reflected defensiveness in the face of a rare show of anger from J. B. After she admitted her failure to register to vote because of her singular school focus, J. B. had spoken harshly to her. Luckily, it was not too late because, despite her claims of supposed apathy, she did care. On election day, she accompanied J. B. to the polls and happily (and proudly) voted a straight Democratic ballot in her first presidential election. Several days later, the winner of the close race was confirmed, and her choice helped Wilson narrowly defeat the Republican candidate, Supreme Court justice Charles Evans Hughes.

Barbe, like many Americans, had voted for Wilson in part because of his promise to keep America out of the war. This vow was not destined to hold, but in early 1917 direct US involvement in the European war was still in the future, and Barbe's main concern was school. Her winter-term classes proved to be as challenging as the fall term and her social schedule just as full. Juna often complained that Barbe was busy every minute, which was true. She was swamped with schoolwork and rarely made it to bed before midnight. Juna worried that Barbe's schedule jeopardized her health, but she also complained about Barbe's inability (or resistance) to housework. For the first time in more than a decade, Juna had to pay someone to help, and she was not happy about this turn of events, thus beginning a long string of hired and fired and much-maligned housekeepers. Nevertheless, the fact that Barbe continued to live with the Lennons throughout this period, despite the tension and her retreat from housework, speaks to her place as part of the family, not merely a "boarder" trading work for food and bed. A health crisis, however, offered an even stronger illustration of Barbe's role in the family.

On March 3, 1917, J. B. checked into the local hospital to have hernia surgery. Late-nineteenth-century adoption of anesthesia as well as disinfection and sterilization techniques had made surgery, in general, less traumatic and dangerous. Plus, by the early twentieth century, hernia procedures were relatively common. Nevertheless, surgery still represented a considerable risk. Outpatient and laparoscopic procedures were many decades in the future, and long postsurgery hospital stays were the norm, so, not surprisingly, seven days after his procedure, J. B. was still in the hospital. He had been on "opiates" for the pain, but his recovery had seemed uneventful when complications arose. On that seventh day, Juna, nearly hysterical, called Barbe to report that J. B. had unexpectedly taken a turn for the worse. Barbe rushed to the hospital to find a roomful of doctors and nurses battling to save his life. For the next week, J. B. battled infection, near kidney failure, and recurring dementia as the doctors attempted to cure him using a variety of treatments, which in hindsight offer reminders of the still relatively primitive state of medicine. These methods included "taking out blood and putting salt water in his arm," putting him in

hot packs, "washing out his stomach," giving him strychnine injec-
tions, and feeding him champagne.[3]

Despite their best efforts, nothing seemed to be working, and
J. B.'s prospects looked so grim that Juna contacted their son (John) to
come in from New York City to say his good-byes. He arrived the next
day, but despite John's presence Juna and Barbe seemed to rely primarily on each other through a precarious and exhausting week. J. B.
would seem better, and then he would become confused, not know
who they were, and have long vomiting spells. Finally, toward the end
of the week, the doctors offered an encouraging report, and J. B. felt
well enough to request ice cream and a cigar, which they supplied. He
would not be sent home until March 29, but Barbe finally felt that
the crisis was over. She could now succumb to her extreme weariness,
and that night she slept in her own bed rather than at J. B.'s bedside
with Juna. And while it was true that the emotional stress abated for
the family, J. B.'s hernia issues continued. In mid-April the doctors
determined the surgery had been a failure. They fitted him for a truss,
and (in what is likely the most shocking part of this saga for modern
readers) his money for the failed operation was returned! This crisis not
only illustrates Barbe's inclusion as family, but it also provides a context
to show how far she had moved beyond her dependent role within
the household. She clearly was part of the Lennon family, but she did
not allow that responsibility to diminish her sense of an individual
identity. The worst of J. B.'s emergency had occurred during a short
break between terms, but during much of his hospital stay she also
continued her classes. Without doubt, the feeling of personal empowerment commonly reported by female college students contributed to
her ability to balance both.

As April 1917 blossomed, J. B. returned home for further recu-
peration, Barbe's spring session turned to summer term, and she con-
templated the end of her full-time status with mixed emotions. On
the one hand, she hated to see this period end. She had thrived in the
academic and social atmosphere of ISNU. A midsummer walk around
the campus with a fellow student inspired her to note "how seldom I
have time to enjoy the beauty of the place."[4] Her affection for ISNU
is clear, but it also hints at other feelings. A full load of classes along

with the accompanying deadlines and exams were time-consuming and could be very stressful. Not surprisingly, she also offered thanks on several occasions that the school term was almost over. As her year leave drew to an end, the Bloomington School Board assured Barbe of a teaching assignment, so although she did not know where she would be, she looked to return to a somewhat familiar routine. But by the time Barbe finished her year at ISNU, she was, as were Americans in general, forced to incorporate a new sense of normal as the United States finally entered the ongoing European war.

Against this new backdrop, Barbe finished her yearlong teaching sabbatical and returned to the head of a classroom in September 1917. Her resumed schedule was both familiar and different. She returned to teaching but at a different school (Franklin) and with an increased desire for classroom autonomy. For example, despite strict guidelines restricting teachers' abilities to alter course materials, she discussed changing an assigned book with Superintendent Stableton and questioned the usefulness of student recitations as a learning tool. Building on the commitment of her yearlong leave, she also chose to take classes at night after teaching during the day. ISNU had also instituted off-campus "extension" sections in 1914, in an effort to provide working teachers increased access to courses. Taking advantage, Barbe took Sociology, Psychology, and Social Problems during the regular school-year terms and then took School Management in the summer term of 1918. She especially enjoyed the Sociology and Social Problems courses, which covered contemporary topics such as rural life and education, the distribution of wealth, marriage and divorce, demographics, industrial education, eugenics, and, in the vernacular of the time, "the woman problem" and "the Negro problem." She continued to thrive on the intellectual challenge but missed ISNU campus life. An invitation to a lunch on campus with school friends brought a rush of nostalgic joy. Her busy schedule also prompted familiar patterns between Barbe and Juna. Barbe complained that Juna was treating her badly, and Juna complained that Barbe devoted too much time to her work as both a teacher and a student. But school responsibilities were not the only commitment drawing her away from home; her involvement in the war effort also played a role.

With millions of men diverted into military service, both business and government relied on women's efforts during the war years. A small number of women served in noncombat positions in the military, but women's biggest impact came from their presence in the paid labor force and the volunteer realm. Record numbers of women became wage earners for the first time, helping to fill both the jobs left empty by mustering soldiers and the new jobs created in the war production industry. Some of the newly acquired factory jobs clearly challenged gendered ideals, but for the most part women's efforts, both paid and volunteer, fell within contemporary society's view of appropriate gendered parameters. They labored as nurses, telephone operators, and clerks; sewed for the Red Cross and other relief efforts; organized fund drives and parades for Liberty Bonds and the Red Cross; planted gardens; and voluntarily conserved meat, sugar, and wheat. The newly formed propaganda arm of the US government (the Committee on Public Information) also emphasized the importance of traditional womanhood by using images of nurturing mothers and innocent young girls as recruiting tools. Nevertheless, even though attitudes, as well as much of women's efforts, were often traditional in scope, they could also offer a context for autonomy and empowerment. This dynamic certainly was true for Barbe.

She participated in Liberty Bond drives and volunteered in a variety of capacities for the Red Cross and the Belgium Relief Fund. Among other things, she "adopted" two refugee boys at Christmas, sending them stockings filled with mittens, chocolate, and other treats. She also served as the secretary of the Junior Red Cross, which had been commissioned by Woodrow Wilson in late 1917. The Junior Red Cross partnered with local Red Cross organizations to provide students an opportunity to support the war effort. By 1919 the group boasted 11 million members and produced nearly 10 percent of the Red Cross's total output. Barbe's leadership skills as a teacher served this effort well, as local Junior Red Cross children undertook many of the same tasks as their mothers and teachers. They made and collected clothes for war victims, produced hospital supplies, and collected money. Barbe's students also contributed to the war effort. She guided them as they endeavored to help refugee children by assembling "Friendship Boxes" filled with cards and clothes. She also oversaw their efforts to make slings, abdominal bandages, shoulder wraps, hot water bottle covers, bed socks, bootees, hoods, and mittens as well as comfort pillows, small quilts, gun wipes, and ration heaters for refugees and soldiers. War work, teaching duties, and her ISNU class schedule kept Barbe very busy, but they also acted to boost her growing sense of independence and competence. The final year of the war brought more change and more opportunity to illustrate her growing autonomy.

But as 1918 opened, this autonomy was temporarily frozen by forces stronger than Barbe's will for independence. The country was hit with bitterly cold record low temperatures and the worst snowfall since 1900. The mood at the Lennon house was tense. Room temperatures in the library and bedrooms rose only to forty-eight degrees, and the chill between Juna and Barbe did not help. In December 1917, J. B. had been appointed as a conciliation commissioner with the US Department of Labor. He was once again on the road, recommending solutions for labor disputes throughout the nation. Juna's declining health kept her from joining him, which left the two women to fall even deeper into their long-standing patterns. The record cold only made matters worse. For weeks the two women were forced to live in the kitchen with both stoves going simply to keep from freezing. Wartime shortages did not help. The US fuel administrator had ordered all stores and factories closed on Mondays in order to conserve fuel and banned coal deliveries to public places, churches, and schools. As a result, schools were closed until the first week of February. Barbe used this break from classes (as both a teacher and a student) to catch up on her reading for her Sociology and Psychology classes, but the stress of the close quarters could be stifling. When the stores opened, she braved the elements and indulged in her still favorite pastime, shopping, while also escaping Juna's presence. She splurged on a new seal muff simply because it matched her coat, but she also wanted to replace older items she had donated to war-relief funds as well as her financially struggling sisters. Finally, in early February, the cold and snow finally abated, and she returned to her now familiar regular schedule of work, school, and volunteering. But in the midst of the

January lockdown, a single letter from an acquaintance in Tulsa escalated to a series of letters, which offered a potentially life-changing path as spring approached.

What prompted this first letter between Barbe and Billie Travis is unknown, but their long-distance liaison quickly grew serious. For the first time since Otto Erdmann had broken her heart, she opened herself up to the idea of a serious relationship. But while she took her time considering her feelings, Travis had already made his decision. In late February, he arranged for the superintendent of Tulsa County schools to send Barbe information on their schools and urged her to apply for a position. Then in late March 1918, he proposed marriage. She did not immediately offer a yes or a no, but he must have assumed that the yes was coming. In April he sent his plan for a five-room bungalow that he hoped to make their home, and in May he relayed a job offer from the Tulsa School District. She clearly had some affection for him, but she remained both privately and publicly reticent about her feelings, perhaps recalling her prior pain. Travis complained about her obvious hesitancy. He chastised her for writing too infrequently, complaining that he received a letter only once or twice a week, as compared to his nearly daily posts. Her response to his worries demonstrates at least one reason she hesitated to commit. She reminded him that while she enjoyed his letters, she was too busy to write him daily. Her priorities clearly did not match his.

Despite this mismatch of priorities, she still had not given his proposal a definitive answer as the school year came to a close. But her actions illustrate she had little intention of uprooting her life for him. On June 8, 1918, she signed a contract with the Bloomington School District for the fall semester (receiving a raise of ten dollars, taking her to ninety dollars per month) and then went to ISNU and planned her summer class schedule. Her career, not marriage, clearly was forefront in her mind. The decision, however, was sealed the following week. She received a letter (from a person unnamed in her journal) that was not favorable to Travis. She never articulated the letter's details, and it is not clear whether she (or perhaps Juna or J. B.) instigated some sort of "investigation" or whether a friend simply passed on unsolicited information. It is easy to imagine a newly independent Barbe taking personal precautions so as not to endure another surprise marriage announcement. It is also easy to imagine the Lennons neither trusting the veracity of this long-distance Lothario nor wanting Barbe to move to Tulsa. Evidence for J. B.'s involvement, perhaps, survives in his daily expense log for his work for the Department of Labor. This log contains the name and address of only one person, a William Travis of Tulsa, Oklahoma, so J. B. may have had a hand in this "investigation." Regardless of the details, this news put an end to any marriage consideration Barbe may have harbored. Billie Travis claimed that the wrong Travis had been investigated and that he still loved her and wanted to move past this incident. Barbe claimed disappointment in the outcome, but she was unmoved by his pleas of mistaken identity. The two continued to correspond periodically, so the "not favorable" could not have been too horrifying, but Barbe never wavered from the definitive no she gave to both Travis and the Tulsa School Board.

Travis had never risen to the top of her priority list, so her busy schedule had continued with little change both during and after their relationship. She taught, matriculated, and volunteered. She kept abreast of current events. For example, that spring she had attended director of the federal Children's Bureau Julia Lathrop's lecture "War and Our Children" and William Jennings Bryan's talk on temperance. Bryan's lecture anticipated another local-option vote, which in April again took the town dry (reversing a wet vote several years prior that had reversed a previous dry vote). Once the temperatures rose and the snow melted, Juna and Barbe's tiffs returned to the familiar, but now escalating, battle to find acceptable household help. Juna would hire a housekeeper, find fault, and then expect Barbe to fire her. They went through Mrs. Traugh, Irene, Cora, Esther, Ethel, and Annie in the space of a year. Apparently, the house got a bit of a reputation, as they finally resorted to "blind ads" to find new help. Juna then changed strategies and brought home a young woman who, like Barbe nearly twenty years prior, attended school but helped with the housework in lieu of paying for room and board. Barbe felt a bit threatened regarding the prospect of someone replacing her in the Lennon family. Nevertheless, the same level of confidence that allowed her to step confidently away from a marriage proposal allowed her to fret (and claim private satisfaction when the girl did not work out) but not obsess over her potential banishment, as she would have done in the past. This maturity was also evident in her decision to accept a professional opportunity proffered in the fall of 1918.

In early August, Barbe's self-improvement efforts paid off when the superintendent offered her a job as the principal of the Sarah Raymond School. She briefly hesitated because she loved her school and fellow colleagues and hated the thought of leaving Franklin. But this was a proposal to which she could commit. After taking only the night to think it over (and again apparently without consulting family or friends), she accepted the position the next morning. Her experience as a teacher as well as her ISNU studies in school management served her well in a challenging position that combined both aspects. According to the "rules," as a teaching principal she was responsible for teaching a class, but she was also charged with making sure that the rules and regulations of the Board of Education were observed and enforced at her school. These required duties ranged from the ringing of the school bells, overseeing fire drills, and ordering supplies to determining all questions of discipline, submitting student and facility status reports, and making out payrolls. Meetings—with other principals, supervisors, and teachers as well as the Mothers Club—become an ever bigger part of Barbe's week as well. Principals' salaries were based on the number of teachers supervised. Sarah Raymond was the smallest school in Bloomington, so this promotion garnered her $104 per month, only $14 more than she would have earned teaching that year. Despite the low pay, she was enthusiastic about the new challenge and its potential.

Barbe's tenure as a principal began the first week of September 1918 with a meeting of city principals. Three weeks later, September ended with another principals' meeting and a positive performance review from her superintendent. As October opened, her biggest concern was an outbreak of mumps keeping several students out of school. But her short journal notation on the second day of October provides a preview of a different health crisis that for nearly a month threatened to overpower even the war news: "Spanish influenza has started here—one death today."[5] This particularly deadly strain of flu had first appeared in early 1918, and before it ended in 1920 almost 30 percent of the world's population would be affected. An estimated 50 to 70 million people died worldwide. Nearly 700,000 people succumbed in the United States alone. The October outbreak changed Barbe's daily routine, as Bloomington attempted to mitigate risk. On October 10, 1918, after a week of stressing calm, the Board of Health ordered public gatherings closed. Initially, schools were exempt from that order, but the following day schools were also shut down. Despite precautions, the number of local influenza cases continued to rise. Every few days, Barbe made note of a friend's or colleague's sickness or death. As the death toll rose, ideas calculated to calm growing fears emerged from a host of sources. Mandates from government agencies, such as making spitting in public illegal and requiring the burning of all "discharges," were designed to lower the chances of spreading infection. Punditry advice ranged from common sense (avoid crowds) to potentially confusing (chew your food). Even mourning rituals were affected. Funerals had to be outside, as they were not allowed in houses or chapels. The specter of the flu consumed much of the town's attention.

Despite the fact that influenza news vied with war news for supremacy and flu restrictions limited most activities, the war and its needs could not be ignored. This reality provided Barbe a chance to serve the war effort in a different capacity than her past volunteering roles. The Board of Health "suggested" that while school was suspended, local teachers would be perfect substitutes to step in as volunteer nurses. They based this notion on the assumption that both were essentially nurturing female roles. But Barbe as well as numerous other teachers chose another avenue instead. In September the Selective Service Act had widened the draft-registration age requirements to include all men aged eighteen to forty-five (from the previous span of twenty-one to thirty-one). The expanded age rules led to a surge of registers whose eligibility to serve was to be determined by local Exemption Boards. The boards, usually filled by local dignitaries, ranked potential draftees based on several factors, including physical status, occupation, dependency status, and religious objections. During the school closure, Barbe and several other teachers worked at the courthouse nearly every day, providing support as the local Exemption Board processed the rush of registers. But as October turned to November, things looked to be returning to normal, albeit wartime normal. On October 31, 1918, the *Pantagraph* reported that the epidemic had subsided. In reality it would return several times over the next six months, but in numbers the worst days had passed. Over the next few days, most of the gathering bans were lifted, and on November 4, 1918, schools started back up. Barbe prepared to resume her wartime routine as principal, teacher, student, and Red Cross volunteer, but two events disrupted her plans, one tragedy and one victory.

Three days after classes resumed, Barbe received word that her youngest sister had died suddenly that morning. This aspect of the flu was typical. Along with targeting the young and healthy in disproportionate numbers, it could be tricky. A person could be at work or school in the morning and be dead by nightfall or seem on the mend and then abruptly take a turn and succumb. Barbe took the train to Odell that night and spent the next two days with her family as they buried their youngest surviving daughter. Barbe was gratified by the show of support from much of the community, but she was also disgusted by the drunkenness demonstrated by some of her family, including her father, who (much to Barbe's anger) did not even go to his daughter's funeral. After spending several days with the extended family, she returned to Bloomington just in time for the victory announcement. On November 11, 1918, the Armistice was declared. Schools once again were closed, but this time for a celebration, as mobs of shouting people took to the streets to share their joy. Although it would take months (and for some countries years) to work out official formalities ending the war, for most civilians this day marked the beginning of attempts to return to normal life. Soldiers quickly came home, and businesses and communities rerouted their focus from the war to the desire for "normalcy." Barbe's life resumed much of its former regularity, but, unbeknownst to her, path-changing events were on the horizon.

5

From New Woman at Work
to New Woman at Home,
1919–1921

If Barbe's much-used Kodak camera could have captured one snap-shot encapsulating her life only two years later, her 1919 self may have scarcely recognized that 1921 image. The same could have been said for American society as a whole. When 1919 began, the war was won, and two high-profile progressive goals also moved toward victory. The Eighteenth Amendment banning the sale and distribution of alcohol would take effect in early January 1920, and in August 1920 the Nineteenth Amendment granting universal female suffrage would be ratified. But 1919 also brought a resurgent conservative movement, which branded many progressive reforms as dangerous and un-American. They pointed to the violent excesses of the recent Russian Revolution as proof of the threat and, among other targets, aggressively condemned unions as foreign entities incompatible with American democracy. This attitude combined with widespread labor unrest dealt a nearly fatal blow to the progressive union movement. The contradictions between the success of both progressive and conservative forces provides an apt view of the early 1920s. By 1921 the nation had largely retreated from a commitment to massive social change in exchange for the hope of a return to "normalcy;" yet what normal meant was not always clear, for modernity and conservatism wrangled for preeminence in American society. For women these contradictions existed side by side in the 1920s New Woman. She could be a single, independent, and adventuresome working woman, but the assumption of future marriage and motherhood shaped her opportunities and challenges. Barbe's postwar experiences illustrate this dynamic.

Both her college and her war-work experiences had augmented Barbe's expanding sense of autonomy. In the months after Armistice Day, her life resumed much of its former regularity, without sacrificing continued independent growth. As 1919 moved forward, she fulfilled her time-consuming and varying responsibilities as principal and teacher, resumed her ISNU extension classes, and spent her limited free time mostly with friends. Billie Travis reenergized his efforts to woo Barbe back, but she still resisted. And she and Juna continued their contentious struggles over housekeeping and time management. But her increasing personal and professional autonomy also added new outlets. She was asked to take over the superintendency of the Unitarian Sunday School, voted into the Women's Chamber of Commerce, made a voting member of the local Mothers Club, and expanded her time commitment to the local branch of the Illinois State Teachers Association (ISTA). The ISTA (the future Illinois Education Association) had organized in the 1850s, but the Central Illinois Teachers Association had not become an official affiliate until 1912. At that time, they voted to adopt the ISTA's reorganization plan, and the previously largely autonomous Central Illinois Teachers Association transformed into one of seven divisions (the Central Division) of the newly revamped statewide organization. In the fall of 1914, about the same time as Barbe became enamored with Otto Erdmann, these newly affiliated downstate divisions used their united numbers to escalate their efforts for pension protection.

The Illinois pension fight was not a new one. Thanks to the fierce lobbying of Chicago teachers, Illinois had passed enabling legislation for a pension law in 1895. Unfortunately, nearly two decades later, only Chicago teachers had benefited from the law. By 1914 other Illinois teachers had escalated their demands for the same rights. In

December 1914, Barbe's local McLean County schools' newsletter argued the teachers' position, citing (among other reasons) low salaries and nearly nonexistent wage increases. According to this polemic, over a ten-year period the average postal worker would bring home an aggregate total more than twice the money earned by an average grade school teacher ($11,000 as compared to $5,259). Even school janitors earned higher wages than the teachers working in the same building. Factoring in the degree of education recently mandated by teacher certification laws, which were not prerequisites of the other higher-paying jobs, and the inequity became even more apparent. The author concluded that if schools were unable or unwilling to pay teachers decent salaries, then at least they could provide a pension program. Legislators finally responded to teachers' demands in July 1915, with the first statewide teacher pension plan. It was a start, but a rather inadequate one, as it allotted a mere $400 per year benefit after twenty-five years of service. Barbe had kept abreast of this pension fight, but with her focus first on Erdmann and then ISNU, she had taken no active part in the lobby. But her confidence as well as her assumptions about her future had altered considerably since 1914, so when politicians threatened in 1919 to defund teacher pensions, she stepped into the fight. She helped organize meetings, reached out to local merchants for support, and drafted letters and petitions for submission to the Illinois legislators. Their efforts succeeded in halting those calls for defunding, but it would not be the last time they had to fight that fight. Between their ongoing battle to raise benefits and the periodic need to deflect those calling for further fund reductions, their pension woes would drag on for decades.

During this period, teachers were not just looking to secure their futures; they also endeavored to improve their present. Barbe also joined that fight, which ironically had to start within the education association before it could look outward. By 1917 the ISTA's rapid membership growth had led leaders to instigate a delegate system of representation. This decision was prompted, in part, by the fact that female classroom teachers made up a substantial portion of the membership, while the mostly male administrators were in the minority. The organization needed the teachers' support to succeed, but the administrators feared the former's greater numbers endangered the latter's ability to hold tight to leadership positions. Now (largely male) regional division leaders appointed a limited number of voting delegates, thus eliminating the possibility of teachers voting en masse against the interests of leadership, which often differed significantly from teachers. In particular, administrators sought to raise their profile to the level of other Progressive Era professionals. To that end, they focused closely on establishing standards of professionalization rather than on a hands-on approach regarding improving curricular and teaching strategies. In an attempt to redirect some focus back to their challenges, classroom teachers bypassed the leadership and organized their own subsections within the ISTA divisions. Barbe's promotion to teaching principal had expanded her administrative responsibilities, but she still largely identified as a teacher. This sense of identity was clear at the mid-April 1919 annual meeting of the ISTA–Central Division when Barbe helped organized a pilot section of "intermediate grade" teachers. As the elected secretary of this group, she helped formulate its mission to tackle the day-to-day issues faced by midlevel classroom teachers and push for official ISTA recognition. As April 1919 drew to a close, these efforts indicate she was focused on continued professional and personal empowerment.

Despite this growth, however, her complicated relationship with Juna also continued to hold emotional sway. Barbe resisted Juna's efforts at control, but, in reality, Juna's opinion mattered, and she still had the power to affect Barbe's state of mind. An early May 1919 exchange illustrates this truth. In her typical fashion, Juna berated Barbe over supper. She warned Barbe that her constant working and worrying about work were hazardous to her health. Barbe privately acknowledged that she was indeed very tired but rebuffed Juna and bristled at the comments. After nineteen years of struggle, their relationship seemed destined to never reach smooth waters. Then only hours after this fight, Juna suffered a heart attack. Knowing that she was dying, Juna endeavored to calm the rough seas that had largely defined their relationship and used her final words to tell Barbe that "she had always loved me like her own daughter." Barbe was devastated by the loss but found real solace in Juna's long-desired and clear declaration of love and familial membership. Both Juna's words and Barbe's gratitude for them provide a glimpse into the heart of the women's complex relationship. Their relationship also gave rise to Barbe's next decision, when only moments before Juna's funeral she said yes to J. B.'s request that she "stay and make a home for him." Whether J. B. was aware that this agreement was, at least in part, the result of a promise Barbe had made to Juna the prior summer is unknown. But this promise to care for J. B. in the event of Juna's death ultimately changed Barbe's life.[1]

The eventual results would take some time to completely manifest, but the commitment itself led to immediate tension, as Barbe attempted to balance her feelings of loyalty with her continued desire for autonomy. Nonetheless, in the aftermath of the tragedy, she proved herself worthy of Juna's trust. Despite the presence of other friends and family, including J. B. and Juna's son, John, J. B. depended on Barbe for pragmatic as well as emotional support. She helped him pick out the casket before the funeral and was by his side throughout. After the funeral John left, and her care extended into the following weeks. She accompanied J. B. to the courthouse to swear to the signatures in Juna's will, attended Presbyterian church services in lieu of the Unitarian, wrote thank-you cards to all who had sent flowers, gathered up the personal items Juna had promised to others, packed away Juna's dresses, and cleaned out her bureau. J. B. also quickly took steps to allow for Barbe's expanded role in the house by opening up a bank account so that she could pay house bills via check. Given her longtime membership in the Lennon family home, Barbe's continued assistance, even without her promise to Juna, was not unexpected. It simply echoed a prevailing societal belief. Despite the growing acceptance of single working women, most people still assumed that a woman's true calling was as family caretaker, whether as daughter, sister, wife, or mother. Barbe felt a sense of familial responsibility but still struggled with that assumption. Less than two weeks after Juna's death, she turned to her former superintendent for advice. In the fifteen years since she had joined the Bloomington School District, he had become a mentor as well as a family friend. His reaction left no room for ambiguity. It was Barbe's duty to step up and "keep house" for J. B.

But even given the assurances of someone she trusted and her own feelings of responsibility, Barbe still struggled. Her strong sense of family loyalty and the burden of societal assumptions clashed with her desire to maintain a sense of autonomy. Initially, she tried to balance her independent life and J. B.'s needs. She returned to the classroom the week after the funeral. It was difficult, but the students were kind and teaching quickly resumed its sense of routine. She also returned to the classroom on the other side of the chalk as an ISNU student. Her sociology extension course, which focused on the contemporary status of immigrants, African Americans, and women, provided distraction from her own dilemmas. Despite everything else, her determination to pursue education still prevailed, and only weeks after Juna's funeral she completed the course with a final grade of 90 percent. Unbeknownst to her at the time, this class would be her last one for nearly a decade. As the months wore on, her efforts to maintain her separate life as well as many of her prior outside commitments became more difficult. She grew increasingly exhausted as she struggled to carry her multiple responsibilities along with the weight of the mantel of guilt she wore whenever she left J. B. alone at home.

Barbe's emotions had continued to be conflicted, as she worried about the effect her return to work had on J. B., especially given that as a woman, she could have stepped away from her job without societal judgment. In contrast, J. B.'s resumption of outside duties was assumed even if he was conflicted. Only three weeks after Juna's death, he traveled to Atlantic City, where he joined fellow AFL labor leaders as they debated the merits of the proposed Prohibition amendment, the League of Nations, and allowing African American laborers greater access to unions. This setting offered potential strife for the grieving widower. He was still held in high regards among many labor reformers, but he no longer held an official position with the AFL. Plus, he and AFL president Samuel Gompers increasingly viewed future reform differently. In recent years, J. B. had publicly supported, or at least considered the merits of, positions Gompers considered somewhat radical, such as nationalizing railroads, municipalizing public utilities, guaranteeing civil liberties, and expanding civil rights. In addition, J. B. had stepped out on his own politically. In April 1919, J. B. had narrowly lost a bid as mayor on the "Bloomington Labor Party" ticket. This local slate was part of a wider effort to form a national labor party. Always mindful of political fallout, Gompers opposed this effort as well as the formation later that year of the Illinois Farm Labor Party (an amalgamation of laborers, socialists, Bull Moose progressives, and disgruntled farmers) for which J. B. would run (and again lose) a 1920 bid as state treasurer.

Friend and fellow national labor leader James Duncan wrote J. B. in the aftermath of the AFL convention, and his letter served as a follow-up to their previous discussion regarding their mutual and growing dissatisfaction with Gompers's hubris and conservatism. Both men were frustrated with Gompers's direction, and Duncan's presence at the convention no doubt had offered some support during this first and potentially tense foray back into work. But J. B. also turned to Barbe for support in completing this venture. Only days after he left home, she received a letter in which he pleaded for her company. This plea prompted her decision to join him for the remaining three weeks of his stay. She attended many of the sessions as a spectator, but she also enjoyed Atlantic City's many amusements: riding the "boardwalk chairs," walking on the beach, plunging in the ocean, watching the fish hauls, and attending vaudeville shows. At the end of June, the two returned to Bloomington together, and, in the aftermath of this shared trip, something happened that potentially mapped out her future. Although the clues are sparse and conclusions regarding what that "something" was are speculation, they bear consideration.

Barbe's June 1919 journal entries are mostly mundane, but a June 29 notation raises questions. The body of the entry is not the puzzle. She simply remarked that J. B. was at a meeting and was late for dinner. But at the top of this page, written in the header, is the word *proposal*. This notation clearly was added at some point after that day's entry and is consistent with her habit of commemorating a date she later decided was important. (For example, the same sort of after-the-fact notation occurred to highlight the first day that she met Otto Erdmann.) In addition, from June 24 through July 10, either an

X or *XX* appears next to the date. A single dash sets July 11 off and then nothing until an *X* appears for July 22 through July 24. It is not clear what these marks signify. Female journal writers commonly use symbols to keep track of menstrual cycles (and she did comment on July 26 that she was "just over being under the weather") or sexual encounters. But given these few dates are the only times these marks appear in a set of journals spanning multiple decades, it is difficult to make either one of those leaps. The speculation deepens when J. B.'s Department of Labor expense log is considered. Its sole purpose was as a log for travel reimbursement for his ongoing Department of Labor work. It details his daily location for more than three years but contains no personal commentary. A typical entry included the date followed simply by "at home" or "left Bloomington" or "arrived in Hammond," so the notation of "all day in Bloomington (Barbara)" for the span of July 7 through July 14, 1919, like Barbe's mysterious marks, was an anomaly.[2]

What, if any, conclusions can be drawn from these vague clues? If we factor in the knowledge that in the first week of June 1920 (just over one year after Juna's death), Barbe notes with no fanfare or background "decided to marry in two weeks," then the conclusion that "proposal" meant a discussion regarding the possibility of the two marrying in a year's time (the customary period of mourning) is not a farfetched one. Whether this discussion was prompted by J. B.'s fear that Barbe's desire for autonomy would lead her away or because of a sexual encounter or out of their shared affection or something else cannot be known. But other entries from this period add fuel to the speculation regarding the nature of their relationship. On the night of June 30 (the day after the "proposal"), Barbe had trouble sleeping, perhaps pondering this "proposal." A strain seemed to hover over the week. On the Fourth of July, the two went to Miller Park to watch the fireworks, but after walking home they quarreled. J. B. left for a one-day trip on the sixth but was hesitant to go because he did not want to leave Barbe home alone. J. B., perhaps, was also troubled by the thoughts of good friend and confidant James Duncan. In the same letter in which he addressed Gompers's shortcomings, Duncan noted that he was "mighty glad that Barbara is with you. She is a lady of

good judgment and a pal . . . [who] will be encouraging and helpful."
But he also noted that there is a "mental loftiness to that domestic and
filial thought which supersedes all else."[3]

Perhaps this note contributed to J. B.'s uncertainty as to whether
Barbe should be thought of as a potential bride or a "pal" or if his "filial" responsibilities to his surrogate daughter superseded both of these
categories. What is certain is that their tensions and arguments continued over the summer. In early August, she went riding with friends
and did not return home until 10:15 p.m., finding a very angry J. B.
ready to call the police to find them. Her reaction was also anger. "I
stay home and work and am begrudged any little recreation. Am not
going to be pestered this way. . . . It's wearing me out." The next day,
she tearfully noted that she felt like "going somewhere else to make
my home."[4] Whether J. B. and Barbe had reached any decision about
marriage during those summer months is not clear, but they both
struggled to define their place within the household. They argued
frequently, as he continued to scold her and she continued to chafe
at his attitude. Nevertheless, despite her exhaustion, the continued
friction, and occasional threats to move out, she showed no real signs
of leaving. Instead, she continued to take on the bulk of the duties of
the "woman of the house" while also attempting to maintain a sem-
blance of her own independence. This proved increasingly difficult.
The labor and time needed to meet the expectations for a middle-class
household in the 1920s could easily consume the entire week. These
duties were difficult enough without the addition of a full-time job,
which is exactly what September brought. The effort to balance her
work, the house, and the separate life she had been building over the
past few years proved remarkably challenging.

Barbe's growing disenchantment with their arrangement likely
was obvious; plus, J. B. may have realized (as his own veil of grief
cleared) that he had also been difficult, because as the summer drew
to a close he changed his approach. In the aftermath of one of their
many quarrels, he purchased her a 1919 Mitchell touring car from a
local union dealer. Barbe's yearly salary remained under $1,000, and
the Mitchell retailed at more than $1,200 (considerably more than
the $525 price tag of the popular 1919 Ford Model T), so it was an

extraordinarily generous personal gift. Cars were not new to America, but it was not until the 1920s that they would become a societal norm. Increased production, lower prices, higher wages, and the conclusion of the war led to a rapid rise in ownership, which more than tripled in sheer numbers between 1919 and 1929. The car changed American life forever. Industries that supported rubber, glass, steel, and gasoline production exploded. Road and highway construction connected parts of the country previously off the (railroad) tracks. Buses replaced interurban and trolley systems. Roadside restaurants, motels, and gas stations popped up to provide service to the flocks of families heading to new tourist attractions and destinations. In short, a car meant freedom in an entirely new fashion. This expansion of potential freedom proved especially true for women, as the car allowed them a wider scope and less publicly visible means of movement.

She embraced its potential enthusiastically. Within a day of the purchase, Barbe had her first operating and driving lesson, and she was hooked, dubbing her new form of transport "Sallie." This passion seemed a necessary component, because the freedom the car brought was countered by the unreliability of the machine, the roads, and the available services. The fact that the barn door was too narrow to accommodate the car was just the beginning of a litany of nearly constant issues. For example, an early-morning drive with four girlfriends was planned, only to find that before departing she would have to first inflate a tire and put water into the battery. The next day the car was unresponsive, so a local garage picked it up and supposedly repaired the battery. After paying for the repairs and the storage fee, she took the car home, only to discover the next day that once again the car would not start. She got help from a neighbor, and after an hour of cranking they finally got "her" (the car) started so it could be taken to a garage to have a new battery installed. These kinds of maintenance and repair problems were nearly constant, but even when the car operated correctly challenges to its usefulness existed.

Thanks to a 1916 federal aid highway program (and then the more complete Federal Highway Act of 1921), new and improved roads were in the works, but in 1920 many of these changes were still in the future. Another road trip in August 1920 highlights the frustration of this fact. Unpaved roads were still the norm, and they produced so much thick dust that driving could be far from pleasant. Unpaved roads also meant ruts in dry conditions and mud when it was wet, both of which led to the constant threat, and often reality, of getting stuck, breaking something, or blowing a tire. Every stop produced advice from a local "expert" about which trail was the best to avoid these threats. So drivers frequently chose a longer detour on a rumored better road. All of these factors played a role on this August road trip. Detours, bad roads, and time lost trying to find the "Meridian trail" resulted in the roughly 120-mile trip from a friend's home in Greenup back home to Bloomington stretching to more than 130 miles. Slow driving speeds and numerous unplanned stops also played a part in turning their intended pleasurable morning drive into a dusty ten-hour trek. Despite these challenges, Barbe (like many Americans) remained firmly committed to "Sallie," and it continued to play an important role in her independence for years to come.

But in September 1919, a new school year was beginning, and that hopeful independence continued to be complicated by her sense of duty to J. B. She chose to withdraw from a planned ISNU extension class, but she did resume the bulk of her other planned activities. She returned to her prior teaching and administrative workload as well as her commitments to the ISTA, YWCA, Woman's Chamber of Commerce, and Alliance as well as adding a position on the Unitarian Ways and Means Finance Committee. She also saw her friends more frequently than she had during the summer. But J. B.'s efforts to gain favor did not end with the purchase of the car. Throughout the school year, he continued his shows of appreciation and affection, beginning in September with a gift of an ivory mirror, brush, and comb set for her birthday and culminating in May 1920 with a wristwatch to commemorate the end of the school year. His efforts seemed to work, as the two fought less and spent more fun time together. Barbe took J. B. on car rides, and he took her to dinners, movies, and lectures. His work with the Conciliation Commission had ended, but he had been appointed to another Department of Labor position, so he still traveled frequently. But now that things were less stressful, she once again hated to see him go, as the house seemed empty and lonesome when he was away. He also tried to help with the house upkeep and ultimately hired a housekeeper. Contrary to the drama of Juna's string of unsatisfactory housekeepers, they both were pleased when she proved to be both an asset and a pleasant addition to the home. But even given J. B.'s support, the hired help, and the lessening tension, Barbe still felt torn and tired. An early May 1920 journal entry succinctly sums up her complaints regarding the year since Juna's death: "A hard day. Feel as tho I can't go on like this any longer. Teaching and running a house is beyond me."[5]

Despite her exhaustion, as the school year drew to a close, nothing indicates she had any major changes planned. Instead, she seemed poised to continue her path. Bloomington had recently voted an overwhelming yes on a special tax to help raise teachers' salaries, which had fallen far behind the rapidly escalating cost of living. Barbe calculated the 33 percent increase would raise her salary for the next school year to $143 per month, and she celebrated this news with the purchase of a brown silk hat trimmed with ostrich feathers. She also learned she was being considered as a principal for a bigger school, which along with greater responsibilities would have meant even more money. Her professional activism also continued, and her late-spring 1920 activities mirrored those of a year prior. In April 1920, she was reelected secretary of the now official ISTA Intermediate Grades Section of Teachers. The precarious pension system was at risk again, and she again helped draft and gain signatures for another petition to protest negative legislative proposals. She also helped organize a committee tasked with responding to the rumored pension threats posed by the new Illinois Constitutional Convention. But she also took proactive steps to protect her own future financial well-being by purchasing an annuity. None of these actions seem the path of someone planning to be married. Yet on June 9, 1920, after commenting on the hot weather and the fact that she washed the dining room walls and polished the furniture, she added, almost as an afterthought, "Decided last night to be married two weeks from today. Want to get strawberries and cherries put up before we leave."[6]

By the 1920s, both modernism and conservatism worked to shape shifting views on marriage. Social norms in which marriage served primarily as a fundamental pillar of family, community, and societal stability endured, but popular culture, in particular, also increasingly emphasized the necessity of emotional connection, romance, and intimacy between the couple. Barbe's casual mention of their impending marriage was not exactly the most romantic notation, but pragmatism does not necessarily preclude romance. For J. B., the choice to remarry was not surprising. In the 1920s, men commonly, and at much higher rates than women, remarried after the death of a spouse. At seventy years old, he was also of a generation and age where marrying for companionship, and housekeeping, rather than love would not have been surprising. That being said, he clearly had affection for Barbe, and subsequent efforts to secure her future indicate a deep well of feeling. For women, the 1920s brought rising marriage rates, even for college-educated women. During the late nineteenth century, societal resistance to the idea of balancing career and family had led about half of those educated women to choose career over marriage. But by the early 1920s, the resistance to this work-marriage compromise had weakened somewhat. Married women still worked in far fewer numbers than single women, but marriage rates for professional women rose considerably.

Like many other facets of her life, Barbe perched on the edge of these changing ideas about marriage, family, and intimacy. Only five years earlier, she had plunged into an intense pool of feelings and hopes regarding her potential future with Otto Erdmann. But now she was approaching forty and no longer such an ingenue. Plus, her relationship with J. B. was far more complicated than a "first love." She had been part of his life for twenty years. She clearly admired and cared for him, but was this affection and devotion akin to the kind of love she may have hoped for in the past? Was their intimacy the kind that popular culture now declared to be the essential element for a modern marriage? It is difficult to say. J. B. had been a father figure since 1900, and she frequently describes J. B. as "father" in her journals, only once using the endearment "my sweetheart" in the week before their marriage. Even after they marry, however, she routinely calls him "Mr. L," so this habit may be less important than it seems to imply. Her entries never veer into the love-struck sentiment common during her obsession with Otto Erdmann, but her attitude after his death in particular indicates that she also had a deep well of feeling for him. So whether their "love" was the stuff of 1920s romance novels or the stuff of Victorian-era duty, they did bring love to the marriage.

Despite the plan for a mid-June ceremony, the ceremony did not take place until July 1, 1920. Perhaps the strawberries were slow to ripen. Regardless of the reason for the delay, they arose at 3:30 a.m. on the first and made their way to Chicago, where a friend and fellow progressive, Chicago minister and Armour Institute founder and president Dr. Frank Gunsaulus, performed the ceremony. They had shared their plans with no one, so after the ceremony Barbe sent a telegraph to a Bloomington friend, asking her to report the news to the local newspaper. The newlyweds then spent two days sightseeing in Chicago before they boarded the *South American* and embarked on a Great Lakes cruise, with stops in Detroit and Mackinac Island. About halfway through their trip, they ran into two friends from home who informed the couple that their marriage news had everyone in Bloomington talking. They returned home on July 19, 1920, and the town gossip must have balanced out in their favor, as the community seemed to adjust to their new status much more easily than Barbe. Friends offered congratulatory dinners and gifts, and a letter from her former school superintendent summed up the prevailing reactions: "It seemed to me to mean so much for the future happiness to both of you and just the right thing."[7] But now that the honeymoon was over, Barbe struggled with the expectations and changes of her new role as "wife."

These changes began immediately. She signed new signature cards at the bank as Barbara Egger Lennon, a move she soon came to realize signified more than just a symbolic name change, and informed the superintendent of schools she would not be returning to the classroom in September. Nonetheless, she clearly did not want to forego that identity entirely, as she also renewed her teaching certificate and would continue to do so throughout the 1920s. But regardless of what that renewal gesture may have meant for her personal sense of identity, September came and school resumed without her. Instead of standing at the head of a class, she began her new role in earnest, and one September day's outing provides ready illustration of what sort of changes came with her new status. She attended a Mothers Club meeting, but she no longer served as a voting representative of the school district; instead, she was a volunteer "patron." As such, the club presented her with a silver cake stand as a wedding gift and appointed her to the Community Council. This group regularly discussed areas in which the community and education intersected but only in an advisory capacity. After this meeting, she walked to Franklin Square to see a local convention of the newly nationally incorporated American Legion. She stayed for only a short time, however, because J. B. complained when she was gone for long. As she noted, "Mr. L couldn't stand it. Seems as tho I have to give up all pleasures."[8] This tension intensified as she increasingly took on the duties of social housekeeper while simultaneously chafing from the strictures of wifehood.

She remained active in some of her prior groups, but she took on new responsibilities and added new affiliations as well. She was placed on the Educational Committee for the YWCA, tasked with organizing and finding speakers for a series of ten lectures entitled "Know Your City." She became the vice president of the Unitarian Church and a member of the Board of Trustees. She applied, and was chosen, as one of the community's first female election judges. She also became active in the volunteer philanthropy of the local Wesleyan Guild and Aid Society. But her invitation to join the Bloomington Woman's Club serves as the most significant evidence of her changed position. Juna had been a proud member of this philanthropic social housekeeping group, and despite Barbe's standing as the new (and significantly younger) wife, they welcomed her. In February 1921, they even asked her to serve as the club's recording secretary. Despite their welcoming attitude, Barbe felt hesitant about her place. She privately mulled over accepting the invitation and the subsequent officer's position. She ultimately said yes to both and served as the secretary for several years. Her shifting involvements illustrate her understanding and acceptance of her responsibilities as the socially aware middle-class wife, but other signs point to her continued resistance to giving up her individual identity and previous autonomy.

It is unlikely that Barbe had any real intentions of returning to the classroom full-time, especially given that J. B. proved unsupportive of any type of teaching work for his wife. But Barbe's renewed teaching certificate represented a level of continued resistance to the still prevailing social norms that J. B.'s attitude represented. The idea of married women in the workforce had lost some of its stigma during the Progressive Era. By 1920 just over 20 percent of all wage-earning women were married. But if you looked at all married women, only 10 percent of wives worked. This number would continue to rise over the course of the decade (and beyond), but, in the meantime, economics remained the main driving force. Simply put, the vast majority of married women worked only out of financial necessity. And teachers lagged far behind even these rising numbers. By 1930 the percentage of married working female teachers was only 17 percent, compared to the overall number of almost 30 percent, making them a rather rare commodity.

This divide could be traced to a combination of individual choices, pragmatic realities, and societal assumptions. Because of their assumed "middle-class" status, teachers were more likely to marry into the middle class than many other female wage workers, thus making it financially possible to stop working if desired. But even if this was not the case, society still held a particular and ironic view of a female teacher that made it hard for even a married woman with a financial need to continue teaching. A woman's supposed innate nurturing character made her a perfect teacher as well as a perfect wife and mother. Society still tended to see the ideal performance of motherhood as incompatible with wage work, and local community school boards tended to agree. By 1931 more than 75 percent of all school districts enforced this ideal by specifically banning married women and mothers as teachers. Until 1945 the Bloomington School Board's hiring policy was not to hire married women as full-time teachers. Despite local policies and societal assumptions, Barbe did not immediately abandon her profession. And given the opportunity to substitute teach in the fall of 1920, she eagerly took it.

She very much enjoyed the return to the classroom but was not satisfied with being paid only five dollars. As a seasoned teacher, she felt she deserved to receive more than the minimum rate, but like most aspects of teaching in this era the school board made rules to which teachers had little recourse. For Barbe, this particular complaint would not be an issue again. While she had fumed over the low pay, J. B. strongly objected to her decision to substitute. He claimed to be angry that she had agreed to the two-day substitute stint without talking to him. So when asked to sub again the next week, she talked to him. Much to her dismay, she felt compelled to say no to the offer because J. B. proved to be adamantly against her teaching with or without his prior knowledge. It would be more than eight years before she again stood in front of a classroom.

Nonetheless, in addition to continuing to renew her certificate, she also tried to maintain her teaching connections in other ways. As part of those efforts, in April 1921 she attended the two-day annual meeting of the ISTA–Central Division and spent some enjoyable days with friends and former colleagues. She was under no obligation nor should she have felt any real need to earn credits or widen her knowledge base. She had no plans to return to the classroom. She attended not because she had to but because she wanted to experience a sense of her rapidly disappearing former self. And in some ways, this conference marked the symbolic end to the first half of her life, as only a few months later, on July 3, 1921—almost a year to the day after her marriage—Barbe gave birth to a son.

It is unclear exactly when she became aware of her condition. Neither a home nor doctor's office pregnancy test yet existed; the latter would not become available until the 1930s. In reality, most women still relied on their own experience, body awareness, and the shared wisdom of other women to determine pregnancy at its early stages. Barbe, however, may not have had those options. She had never given birth so may have been largely unaware of what to expect when pregnant. She only infrequently saw her mother and sisters and lacked intimate female friends who had given birth, so that avenue of information was unlikely. And finally, given the fact that she was nearly forty years old, it is possible that her menstrual cycles were not as regular as they had been in the past. Plus, by the 1920s, doctors had implemented strategies to alter that reliance on female networks and instincts. Aggressive measures, by male physicians in particular, had contributed to the rising status of doctors as professionals while also reducing the number of female doctors (as professional organizations and medical schools began blocking women) as well as the prevalence of midwives (as doctors increasingly stressed the need for an "expert," that is, a male physician, during birth). Barbe's not infrequent past visits to various physicians demonstrated her trust in the medical profession, so, no doubt, she was predisposed to defer to their expertise, which is what she did. In November and December, she had complained of indigestion, and the doctor had prescribed some unnamed medicine. Whether she, or the doctor, suspected this indigestion as something more is unknown. Regardless, it was April before visits to two different doctors confirmed she should deliver a child in July 1921.

Once the pregnancy was confirmed, she seemed determined to have everything ready for the new arrival, which she was sure was a girl. During the unusually hot months leading up to the birth, in addition to the usual cooking, cleaning, baking, ironing, and laundry, Barbe sewed numerous dresses for her expected daughter and devoted hours to the house. She washed walls, ceilings, and woodwork; painted screens, shades, doors, and the porch; papered the spare bedroom; planted flowers and a garden; and canned, jellied, and packed raspberries, rhubarb, and apples. On the nearly one-hundred-degree day before she gave birth, she worked in the garden, replanting and hoeing, before going grocery shopping and finishing the ironing. That night she woke at about one o'clock, feeling sick, but spent a busy morning straightening the house before her doctor stopped at the house at noon and informed her it was time to go to the hospital. Before calling a taxi for a ride (as J. B. still could not drive), she made his lunch. Two decades before this point, she undoubtedly would have given birth at home with a midwife, as about half of women still did in 1920 (albeit mostly in rural locales). And two decades later, her doctor-assisted anesthetized birthing experience would be the norm. But regardless of the location and decade, J. B.'s absence from the experience remained typical. He was at home when she delivered their son, just four hours after she arrived at the hospital. He was thrilled with the unexpected news that his newborn child was a boy. Before making his way to the hospital, he stopped at the local newspaper to report the arrival of what he proudly termed a future labor leader, and he proposed several prominent labor figures as namesakes, including Woodrow Wilson, John Mitchell, and James Duncan. Barbe did not like any of his name suggestions but had no alternatives in mind (no doubt because of her certainty that she was having a daughter), so she settled on "Duncan Egger Lennon."

The prevailing obstetric experts (mistakenly) believed that moving too soon after childbirth increased chances of blood clots or uterine prolapse, so Barbe and baby spent the next two weeks in the hospital. Record-breaking temperatures and no air-conditioning, which would not become a common feature for hospitals and businesses for another decade, made sleeping difficult for mother and child. J. B. stopped by briefly each day, and Barbe fretted over whether he was eating and how the heat was affecting him. Other than that, Barbe spent most of her days resting, writing announcements, receiving numerous (largely female) visitors, and nursing Duncan. Baby spent his days sleeping and eating, with only the occasional bout of crying. Mother and son's days continued these patterns until ten days after his birth, when Barbe was allowed more freedom to move about and Duncan was circumcised. By the 1920s, this procedure (like birthing in a hospital) was based on contemporary ideas about health and hygiene and conducted on about half of infant boys. Not unexpectedly, Duncan cried pitifully during the procedure but after being given a "bottle of toddy" slept for several hours. He recovered, and two days later mother and son finally departed, fourteen days and $190 after arriving. In the span of just over two years, the parameters of Barbe's life had completely changed. Marriage had already altered the feasibility of maintaining the autonomy she still desired, and she would quickly discover that the birth of her son would produce a whole new set of exhausting challenges against the backdrop of the 1920s.

6

Motherhood and the New Woman, 1921–1928

Marriage and motherhood changed the trajectory of Barbe's life. Before that shift, she had moved, somewhat steadily, toward real autonomy thanks to a combination of career, involvement in professional and community organizations, time as a student, and effective money management. Now she endeavored to bridge the gap between that autonomy and the boundaries brought by marriage and motherhood, all while contending with the shifting cultural context of the 1920s. Like her new life, the 1920s brought changing ideas about liberties and limitations. Popular visions of this decade center on bootleg gin, flappers, and ostentatious displays of wealth, excess, and freedom. In this vision, the October 1929 crash irrevocably launched the Great Depression and ended the "Roaring Twenties" party. In reality, the decade was far more complicated than that simplistic vision. Illegal liquor, late-night jazz clubs, and dancing the Charleston did add intrigue to the lives of some, but for most people these cultural phenomena scarcely touched their everyday lives. Instead of ostentatious shows of newfound wealth, many middle- and working-class families actually fell deep into debt, as wages failed to keep pace with rapidly rising prices. Instead of donning flapper attire and arriving unescorted to all-night parties, most women incorporated the freedom these cultural icons represented in more subtle ways. Their hemlines may have risen a bit as they considered how their lives as wives and mothers fitted into an emerging sentiment that women should expect a measure of personal fulfillment, autonomy, and equity. This was certainly true for Barbe, as the realities of motherhood and marriage stymied any effort to reclaim remnants of her prior independence.

From the moment she became Barbara Egger Lennon, Barbe had been forced to negotiate the new constraints of her status as a "wife." Legally, a married woman gave up much of her financial autonomy. For nearly twenty years, Barbe had earned her own money and managed her own wages and investments. She still had legal rights to the property and investments she brought into the marriage, but now J. B. had the authority to make the financial decisions for the family unit without her consent, a right she did not share. In a telling indication of her new status, her detailed log of expenses dating back to 1903 terminated in July 1920, the month that the couple married. As their finances merged, she also was increasingly dependent on him for spending money. Now even small purchases had to be approved, and this financial dependency chafed. For example, she wanted to buy a new coat, but J. B. vetoed the purchase, claiming that clothes should be bought only if actually necessary. This was galling, but sometimes the dispute obstructed more than the enjoyment of a favorite pastime. Only a few days after returning from their honeymoon trip, she found out that, unbeknownst to her, J. B. planned to sell the house and had received an offer of sixty-five hundred dollars. Ultimately, the sale fell through, but the fact that she had no control over the outcome troubled her. She also angrily confronted J. B. when she discovered he had denied her access to their shared safe deposit box. He rescinded the order, but the very fact that he had the right to assume her second-class status was the issue. These early confrontations about money frustrated Barbe, but she was no neophyte where finances were concerned. Ultimately, she compromised on many other things, especially after Duncan's birth, but she proved to be less conciliatory when it came to protecting her, and her son's, financial security.

J. B.'s advancing age and changing work status intensified this concern. In October 1921, J. B. turned seventy-two years old. The labor community still held him in high regard, as evidenced by, among other things, his recent place on the state Labor Party ballot. But he no longer held official offices for either the AFL or the JTU, and his most recent position for the Department of Labor would end in November 1921. He remained an influential voice, but due to increasingly frequent bouts with (what apparently was) angina his days of active participation, constant travel, and regular paychecks were all but over. This reality helped to explain J. B.'s attempts to control the present-day budget, but it also increased Barbe's concerns about protecting her future. Duncan was still an infant, but J. B. also had other family. His son John was now almost fifty years old, and John's son (J. B.'s grandson, Jack) was also grown. Barbe had known John his entire adult life, and Jack had spent numerous summer days with "Aunt" Barbe, but they rarely visited after Juna's death. Plus, Barbe's complaints about John's attitude toward J. B. indicate he may have been unhappy about his father's second marriage. All of this led Barbe to worry that if J. B. died, John would make a claim on J. B.'s estate that would leave Barbe and Duncan destitute. J. B. was concerned as well but seemed hesitant to act, perhaps not wanting to alienate his firstborn any further. Regardless, Barbe persisted, and "finally" (in her words) six months after Duncan's birth, J. B. took steps to protect his new family.

In January 1922, he signed his newly drafted last will and testament and declared his priorities and her status in clear and unambiguous language. J. B. made Barbe the executor and sole heir of his estate in a document that also noted his "implicit confidence in her and belief that she will use [the estate] for her support and the support and education of our infant son." To ensure that no questions lingered about his intents regarding his oldest son, the document also clearly stated, "I have left no part of my property . . . to my beloved son John F. Lennon because he is a mature man [and] I have already made substantial gifts to him and also because my estate is not more than sufficient to support my wife [and] son."[1] Barbe's push for her son's protection did not stop there. In the coming year, J. B. would also deed the house to Barbe, despite their banker's claim that it was a complicated process; designate her as beneficiary on his insurance policies; and transfer his small savings to her account. These measures helped to ameliorate one stress on the new mother, but negotiating her financial future represented only one facet of Barbe's often exhausting role as wife and mother.

Throughout those same two years in which Barbe endeavored to protect her financial future, she also struggled with the realities of her present-day duties as a full-time housekeeper and mother. Barbe adored her son and marveled in Duncan's growth and accomplishments, but her two-week stay in the hospital after his birth would be her last real respite. And even in the hospital, she nursed another infant in addition to Duncan. Managing a house in the 1920s required a considerable time commitment. Widespread acceptance of scientific home management ideas (as championed by Barbe's own domestic science training) coupled with the availability of modern and supposedly time-saving electric appliances (such as vacuum cleaners, washing machines, refrigerators, and stoves) were supposed to reduce the drudgery of housework. But a 1929 study revealed that housework still demanded more than fifty-one labor hours per week. Modern amenities raised expectations but did nothing to remove the work from the traditional domain of the "housewife." A successful wife and mother understood that, among other duties, she was expected to keep her house sparkling clean, her family's clothes crisply ironed, and her table laid with hot and nutritious meals three times a day. For new mothers, such as Barbe, laundering mountains of baby clothes and cloth diapers added considerable time to that workload. Household help along with an electric Maytag washing tub complete with the newly introduced agitator system would have made life easier. But, unfortunately, their much-reduced income meant no housekeeper and continued use of the basement washtub and hand wringer. Given the totality of her household responsibilities, it is not surprising that Barbe commonly complained that life was "nothing but work, work, from one week to another."[2]

She had hoped to keep, or return to, many of her prior committee, board, and club commitments after Duncan's birth, but this hope largely failed to materialize. She missed, or turned down, many opportunities because her personal sense of responsibility to J. B. and

Duncan kept her close to home, but she also felt unduly confined
by J. B.'s expectations. On numerous occasions, she complained that
she could not go anywhere without a fight because J. B. believed she
should be at home all the time. Barbe's hopes for greater flexibility
hinged on J. B. taking a greater role as a parent, but with historical
distance it is easy to see that this goal likely was untenable. J. B.'s formative parenting years had taken place in the 1870s and 1880s. By
that point, widely accepted ideas regarding distinctly separate gender
roles meant that fatherhood had come to mean providing material
needs, not emotional or hands-on help. This background did little to
prepare J. B. to care for an infant. The few times Barbe left Duncan
with J. B., she received a frantic call for her return home because he
was at a loss about how to stop Duncan's crying. But if she tried to
offer advice about how to deal with Duncan's needs, J. B. reacted angrily. He did not like to be "schooled." As a whole, J. B.'s inconsistent
good intentions did little to relieve her actual duties and often simply
left her frustrated, tired, and miserable.

To complicate matters, J. B. struggled intermittently throughout
1922 with health issues. Undoubtedly, his growing frailty contributed
to his general nervousness about handling his infant child alone. At
the same time, his occasional heart "episodes" quickly were followed
by apparent full recovery, leaving Barbe to waver between anxiety
about his condition, joy when he quickly bounced back, and irritation
when she felt he used his health to manipulate her actions. This roller
coaster of emotions did little to reduce her exhaustion. On J. B.'s
good days, he tried to maintain involvement with things he considered important outside the home. He spent several days in Cincinnati
at an AFL convention in June 1922, and during the fall months he
continued to attend local union meetings and Masonic gatherings as
well as serving on the Executive Board of the local Boy Scouts. Barbe
supported these outlets, but these pastimes did little to ameliorate her
growing exhaustion, and as the new year of 1923 loomed his health
deteriorated further. He began to have horrific nightmares in which
the house was collapsing and suffered through sleepwalking episodes
that took him out of the house and left him disoriented. Barbe grew
more and more exhausted as she struggled to juggle her day-to-day

responsibilities to her young son with the growing reality of her husband's rapid downturn, which in his final weeks included recurring bouts of dementia in which he became almost like a wild man.

The holidays provided little respite from the sad reality of J. B.'s worsening condition. In the weeks after Christmas, she was forced to enlist the help of neighbors and friends several times to manage his increasingly violent and irrational behavior. Then on January 17, 1923, he succumbed to pneumonia brought on by his failing heart and passed away in his own bed. J. B.'s son John had not visited during J. B.'s final illness. And although he did make an appearance at the service, he all but disappeared from Barbe's and Duncan's lives after J. B.'s death. But other people (temporarily) filled that supportive void. Friends, extended family, J. B.'s many colleagues, and the community at large rallied to honor him. Barbe filled her scrapbook with glowing newspaper tributes and the many letters of condolence she received over the next few months. She was gratified to see J. B.'s legacy acknowledged and uplifted by the show of support. Nonetheless, when the dust settled, she still had to come to terms with the new path set before her. She was now a widowed single mother of a small child thrust into the role of autonomous head of household. The impact of her decisions now carried broader meaning than the sense of individual independence she had craved before and after her marriage. Her choices regarding career, education, activism, and, perhaps most important, financial matters now had to be balanced against the responsibilities of single motherhood.

In the year after J. B. died, Barbe often was consumed by grief. If doubt had existed regarding her depth of feeling toward her late husband, her recurring despondency offers strong evidence of her love. But her role as mother and head of household meant that she had little time to wallow in sorrow. Everywhere she looked, responsibility beckoned. She was the sole person responsible for the care of her son as well as the maintenance of her home, car, yard, and any other issue that might arise. All of these responsibilities required not just time but funds. She was not destitute: she had the house, some investments, and the payouts on several private insurance policies. Nevertheless, this was long before Social Security survivor benefits guaranteed an income safety net. After she divvied up her available funds, her monthly income came to only $65 per month, which was less than half of what her salary would have been if she had remained teaching. This placed her well below the average yearly income of approximately $1,200. Like many facets of Barbe's life, however, her experience during this time actually placed her somewhere between two ends of a spectrum. She hoped to remain within the middle-class strata, but, like many women before and after, the death of her husband had put her in uncertain financial waters.

Circumstances for single mothers could be dire, as avenues to deal with this issue were limited. Women who lost their husbands through death, abandonment, or divorce could sometimes turn to family for shelter and support, but for Barbe this choice was an unlikely one for several reasons. Even in her reduced state, Barbe's financial situation may have been better than her parents'. Plus, given her attitude toward her father, it is doubtful that she would have wanted her son to have prolonged exposure to his drinking and temperament. If a woman's family was unwilling or unable to support a needy mother, then she had to look to other sources for financial aid. Traditionally, private charitable organizations served as one of the few options open to mothers in need, but their willingness to help was often linked to their determination of a woman's moral worthiness. During the Progressive Era, however, middle-class social housekeepers moved to bring this aid under the wing of government reform. They aggressively lobbied for various ameliorative support programs, including government-sponsored "mothers' pensions." In 1911 Illinois had become the first state to pass such legislation, and by the 1920s forty-four states had enacted programs authorizing local governments to provide aid to single mothers with children.

These new mothers' pensions also had their weaknesses. They varied considerably by locale, but, like the earlier charity efforts, the stipends were usually limited to "worthy" mothers as defined by local standards. This allowed communities to ignore the needs of minorities, immigrants, unwed mothers, deserted or divorced women, and women who did not provide "suitable" homes. As a result, these funds most often went to widowed mothers, as their diminished financial status was deemed to be no fault of their own. Nevertheless, even when a mother qualified as "deserving" of help (which the vast majority did not), the aid was rarely sufficient to keep her out of the workforce. For example, in 1919 the maximum benefit for a family of four in Illinois was equivalent to only about $275 per month in twenty-first-century dollars and available only for widowed mothers. In fact, most programs were purposely designed with an inadequate fund outlay so as not to encourage sloth and pauperism, which, according to the ideals of the time, were moral failings in themselves. Although Barbe's financial status after J. B.'s death was somewhat precarious, her property and reserves likely would have left her unqualified for government help even if she had applied, which no evidence indicates that she did. So if family and government aid were not viable answers, what other options did she have?

Many impoverished single mothers turned to wage work, and conceivably Barbe could have done so as well. In reality, however, middle-class mothers with children under eighteen did not choose to work outside the home. It was not a complete anomaly—slightly rising numbers of professional women were choosing to combine motherhood and career—but most mothers worked only out of dire financial need, not personal desire. Barbe may have missed the fulfillment of her career, but societal norms dictated that if she could avoid it, then Duncan's care should not be relegated to others. Women working out of necessity could not avoid this reality, and finding someone to care for their children was a constant challenge. If family was unavailable, women in some communities could now turn to "day nurseries." Progressive Era reformers were responsible for these newly conceived community facilities, designed to help women forced to leave their children when they worked. Day nursery care was not meant for mothers with other options. If Barbe had broken middle-class norms and returned to full-time work, it is still unlikely she ever would have considered leaving Duncan at the Bloomington Day Nursery. The YWCA and the Woman's Club (both of which she was still a member) had led the 1908 drive to open this day nursery. Leaving Duncan there would have symbolized an even bigger break with middle-class norms than a return to work would have. In short, she was not (yet) financially desperate, but she needed to find ways to bring in additional money that did not take her away from Duncan for long periods or destroy her place within her current social strata. So even while she suffered through grief on some days that left her almost inconsolable, she pragmatically moved forward with various strategies to augment the household budget and protect the family's financial and social future.

To that end, she continued her past practice of investing (or re-investing) bond and loan funds as well as insurance payouts in new long-term options. In a time of impressive economic growth, this path seemed to be a smart one for future security. Expenses meant not all funds could be reinvested, but she endeavored to keep immediate needs balanced against the future. On a much smaller scale, she also tried to sell some of J. B.'s things, including his typewriter, clothes, jewelry, and toupee. Washing his clothes, cleaning out his filing cabinet, and reading letters he had written her were painful reminders of his absence. The seldom-worn toupee may have brought a smile, especially if she could conjure up the memory of her first sight of it nearly fifteen years past: "Mr L came home this noon with a wig on his head—looks horrid."[3] But to her disappointment, none of the items brought in as much as she hoped. Seeing an opportunity in the fact that potential storage space had not kept pace with the widening popularity of automobiles, she rented out a piece of her barn to car owners at four dollars per month. Plus, beginning in July 1923 (and continuing over the next few summers), she provided a bedroom and board in her home for visiting teachers taking classes at ISNU. All of these efforts, unfortunately, still left the budget short during a period of steadily rising expenses, so to provide what she hoped was a long-term cash influx she decided to create an upstairs rental apartment. She and J. B. had considered this option before his death, and not long after his estate was probated she moved forward with this plan.

After obtaining several bids for the necessary plumbing, carpentry, furnace, and electric work, she settled on a contractor who tallied her likely costs at twelve hundred dollars. In April 1923, the reconfiguring and remodeling began. Once the actual construction work was done, Barbe still had considerable work to do, including acquiring the necessary furnishings and appliances as well as painting, making curtains, cutting and installing screens, laying a linoleum kitchen floor, and final cleanup. In early June, she could finally begin what would be the frustrating process of finding suitable tenants. She wanted someone with steady income, but because these renters essentially would be living in her home, she shied away from "bachelors" or families with too many children or people who seemed, often for undefinable reasons, suspect. Finally, a month after beginning the search, she found an acceptable family to rent the furnished apartment for forty dollars per month. They arrived in July, only to move out unexpectedly two months later, leaving while Barbe was out of town, owing more than a week's worth of rent. She aggressively pursued this payment for months before she finally received her fourteen dollars on March 4, 1924, a full six months after their surreptitious departure. Unfortunately, this first tenant experience was a template for years to come. Acceptable renters were difficult to find, hard to keep, even harder to get rid of if proven unacceptable, and often slow to pay, and they tended to leave behind messes and damaged property. As time passed, she was forced to lower the rent to find tenants, while the hassles of being a landlord seemed to expand, especially given the scope of her other responsibilities.

The housework had almost always fallen under her purview, but now she also had to shoulder the responsibility for all other facets of their home life. She had to mow the grass, shovel the walks, order the coal, as well as take care of the car. The latter included everything from cleaning, waxing, and changing "Sallie's" oil to actual mechanics. When the car's radiator began to leak, she proudly figured out how to solder it back into working order. House, yard, and car maintenance required considerable time, but those myriad responsibilities paled next to the biggest job she did on her own—parent her son. Emotionally, both mother and son felt J. B.'s absence. Duncan talked to his father's picture and often requested to visit him at the "sumetery." Barbe lamented that J. B. was not around to see Duncan grow, and she often noted how proud of his son he would have been. Barbe's desire to have children had never been obvious. She once defended her resistance to spending more time with J. B. and Juna's grandson by commenting, "I didn't like to be around children after teaching for nine months." But she absolutely doted on her own son.[4] Following the dictates of scientific management as they applied to good mothering, she tried to keep him on a consistent schedule and faithfully kept records of pragmatic health milestones like his first tooth and his first bottle. He did not take to the weaning process happily and often refused to take the bottle. But she also happily documented his first haircut, downtown visit, trolley trip, movie, and "machine" ride. He especially enjoyed the latter, and, in a time before car seats and seat belts, his favorite part of any car trip was hanging over the door so he could watch everything. She was proud of his precociousness and seemed to relish his somewhat wayward and mischievous nature. She clearly loved her son and found a measure of fulfillment as a mother, but that role had not erased her desire to maintain her presence in the wider sphere. Logistically, however, single motherhood made that desire very difficult.

These complications did not keep her from trying, however. She remained involved with a variety of groups. Between 1921 and 1929, the philanthropic Woman's Club, in particular, demanded considerable commitment. She held the office of recording secretary for three years, served five years on the Board of Directors, and then was made the group's first official historian. The Alliance, the YWCA, the A Volonte Club, and her duties as an election judge also vied for her attention. But time for these commitments proved difficult to carve out. Acceptable child care was frequently unavailable even for short periods, often meaning she had to either shirk a meeting or take Duncan with her. If Duncan "behaved nicely," then this did not present a problem, but sometimes his presence could be distracting, as when he demanded repeatedly at a Woman's Club Executive Board meeting, "Let's go home Mrs. Lennon."[5] After that episode, she rarely brought him to Woman's Club meetings, but she did continue to take him to other venues, sometimes enduring tacit complaints regarding his presence. Staying at home had its challenges as well. The years immediately after J. B.'s death proved especially taxing. Duncan had entered toddler age, and he was active and eager to do his favorite thing, which he described as "running away." During their first summer alone, Barbe frequently felt compelled to use a clothesline as a sort of leash when she had to weed or mow or do other outdoor work; otherwise, he ran into the street like a squirrel, risking an accident. Increasing car traffic and an extensive system of interurban trolleys as well as trains meant pedestrian-machine collisions were fairly common, so she was right to worry. But watching him every minute was not feasible, and he was a determined child. He even managed to get out of the house at least twice, at one point climbing out his bedroom window. No wonder she felt tired and worn down.

Plus, his desire to run was not her only concern. She also worried about his health in general. Duncan's rashes, fevers, colds, and digestive issues may not seem alarming to modern readers, but vaccines did not yet exist for childhood diseases such as measles, mumps, chicken pox, whooping cough, diphtheria, smallpox, scarlet fever, and polio. In the 1920s, they still were very common and often deadly. To add to her fears, she had only to look back to the high death tolls of the 1918 epidemic to recall how deadly even the flu could be. She dealt with her apprehensions with frequent visits to various doctors. These many consultations elicited varied responses, not all of them directed at Duncan's actual physical health. One physician advised Barbe to create some distance between herself and her son. According to this doctor, she needed to let him out more so as to "toughen" him up. This sort of attitude regarding the development of a so-called healthy mother-son relationship had become more prevalent in the decade after the war. Apprehension concerning the danger to masculinity posed by modern society had existed for decades, but worries stemming from the war effort had added fuel to this fear.

According to some studies, far too many men had either been designated as "unqualified" by the war draft boards or returned home after military service in a "shell-shocked" status. These findings led some researchers to conclude that the modern man had been emasculated in some way. In order to prevent future losses, the definitive roots of this emasculation needed to be identified and severed. Some pundits claimed those roots clearly originated in early family dynamics and in particular condemned what they deemed overly close mother-son relationships. This represented a significant shift in thinking. For much of the nineteenth century, this bond was considered a natural outcome of a mother's duty to devote her life to her family and a son's duty to revere her sacrifice. In the postwar world, attitudes shifted. Reminiscent of the supposed feminizing effects of women teachers (the so-called woman peril), some experts laid the supposed weakness of modern men on the laps of those nurturing mothers. Close documentation and strict scheduling were already expected facets of the scientific approach to mothering, but now some "experts" also touted the benefits of maternal detachment. In an effort to reduce the harmful effects of intense mother-son attachments, some even went as far as advocating minimal physical contact. The "no-hugs" strategy was supposed to eliminate the coddling behaviors deemed harmful to a boy's development so he could grow into an independent and capable man.

Whether Barbe took any of this extreme strategy to heart is unclear, but regardless of this doctor's thoughts about Barbe's mothering techniques, Duncan did experience real childhood health issues. In 1925 his tonsils were removed, in 1926 the house was quarantined for a month when he contracted whooping cough, and in 1927 he contracted scarlet fever. Barbe clearly had real reason to worry. Plus, throughout his early childhood he suffered through a variety of general respiratory symptoms initially diagnosed only as allergies and then, in September 1924, as asthma. Almost immediately after this diagnosis, Duncan began doctor-prescribed treatments in which he regularly inhaled chlorine gas. In the wake of the world war, researchers within the US Army's Chemical Warfare Service had experimented with modified uses of wartime deadly substances such as chlorine and mustard gas. They posited that nonlethal doses of these gases might act as a remedy for various respiratory illnesses, including bronchitis, whooping cough, and colds. Their initial evidence was inconclusive at best, but even President Calvin Coolidge took several chlorine treatments in 1924 and touted their benefits. Despite the lack of substantiation by army research and the condemnation of its use by numerous nonmilitary researchers, many doctors and hospitals continued chlorine gas therapy for several years, and Duncan used an at-home system to maintain a regular schedule of treatments. According to the Centers for Disease Control, symptoms of chlorine gas poisoning include shortness of breath, coughing, and nausea, the very things that continued to trouble Duncan's health. So like Barbe's earlier use of mercury, Duncan's continued regular treatments over the course of several years (before finally switching to tincture of benzoin in 1927 and then adrenal shots in the 1930s) potentially were far more harmful to Duncan's early health than his mother's so-called coddling.

In the midst of Duncan's health issues, the inconsistency of the apartment rental income clearly indicated that Barbe needed to find another means of augmenting their finances. But Duncan's needs and the lack of consistent and acceptable child care limited her choices. Fortunately, changing times brought a new opportunity. In November 1924, she dipped into her savings to pay a $96.30 deposit and signed a contract as a "corsetiere" for the Spencer Company. In much the same way that twentieth-century stay-at-home mothers sold Avon or Mary Kay, Barbe provided private home consultations. She measured, fitted, and sold intimate apparel such as corsets, bras, and sanitary napkin belts. Barbe entered this business at a unique time. In the 1920s, women's dresses became shorter and looser and no longer required traditional corsets. Plus, the economy had experienced a short-term downturn immediately after the war. This collision of economics and fashion produced a dip in sales. The industry had responded with updated products and a new marketing strategy. These shifts saved the industry and altered the perceived role of their sales staff.

A 1925 publication entitled *The Principles of Scientific Corset Fitting* summed up both facets of this shift: "Today corsets are scientifically designed and must be scientifically fitted."[6] No longer should a woman simply purchase her intimate apparel over the counter; instead, they needed to be fitted by a professionally trained corsetiere. The era's faith in experts helped support a view in which a properly fitted undergarment contributed to women's health and general well-being. Doctors even recommended professional corset fittings for female patients as part of their overall approach to healthy living. As a result, corset saleswomen experienced a rise in status and prestige. They were not merely shopgirls or clerks; they were professionals with intimate access to women's lives. Plus, the required deposit Barbe paid in order to contract with the Spencer Corset Company was more money than many working-class women would have earned in a month. Clearly, this necessary outlay helped to keep the sales field to the desired demographic. Throughout the remainder of the decade, Barbe used the connections she had established through her years as an educator and as a member of various women's groups as well as doctors' referrals to establish a customer base. Monthly quotas still were a struggle, but despite that fact she contracted with a second company (Berger Brothers) as well. Two companies increased the stress of meeting quotas, but the job's flexibility and social acceptability countered the less than hoped for income. She would remain under contract to both companies throughout the 1920s and into the 1930s.

This part-time job became the last component of the balancing act that defined the four years after J. B.'s death. Barbe's efforts to juggle her roles as mother and landlord and social housekeeper and corsetiere often left her feeling overwhelmed and unwell. She regularly saw various medical doctors, but in her quest to relieve her symptoms she often also turned to a local osteopath. Osteopathy had been pioneered in the early twentieth century by an American doctor seeking to offer an integrative approach to medicine that emphasized the interconnection between mind, body, and spirit. Its practitioners believed that the body, if provided with the appropriate help, had the ability to heal itself without traditional invasive medical interventions. Osteopathic treatments often involved "setting" or "realigning" parts of the body in much the same way that a chiropractor or physical therapist might today. This integrative approach no doubt had some positive effects, but it also lent itself to the inclusion of possibly fraudulent therapies as evidenced by the enthusiastic adoption of something called "Abrams treatments" by many osteopaths.

Part of an early-twentieth-century trend, American physician Albert Abrams claimed to have discovered how to cure a variety of diseases and general ailments using modern technology. According to his theory, every disease vibrated at a unique wave, so it could be diagnosed and eliminated with his invention: the oscilloclast. Modern technologies still were new enough that many people attributed positive and negative traits to radio waves and electricity that were far beyond their actual applications. Similar to the acceptance of chlorine gas by numerous medical professionals, many osteopaths bought into this "revolutionary" idea, which incorporated their core beliefs regarding the interconnection between mind and body. Diagnosis could even be made long distance with just a drop of blood, enabling the oscilloclast to be sold directly to consumers as well as to osteopathic practitioners. Sales always included an agreement that the sealed electronic box was not to be opened or it would be rendered useless. Not surprisingly, if the box was unsealed, the buyer would find that it was little more than a circuit breaker in a sealed box with an attached rheostat. Thousands upon thousands of people bought into the hopeful power of this "modern" device, including Barbe, who took a series of Abrams treatments, as recommended by her osteopath. The treatments held no actual medicinal benefits, but unlike mercury or chlorine they did not cause physical harm, so in retrospect they likely were harmless except to her budget. And on the plus side, the placebo effect may have relieved stress, which could have contributed to a feeling of well-being, a feeling she needed as her life grew even more complicated.

When Barbe celebrated her birthday in September 1926, Duncan had recently passed his fifth birthday, and the fourth anniversary of J. B.'s death loomed. She remained head of household, mother, landlord, corsetiere, club member, and election judge, but she also looked to make some changes. Duncan had finally reached school age, and in early November 1926 he entered kindergarten at the ISNU Metcalf laboratory school. Barbe decided to take advantage of his half day in school to return to school as well. She had never let go of her goal of earning her ISNU diploma, and she decided that now was the time. By this point, ISNU had merged the previously separate "Normal School" and "Teacher's College" into one system that offered a variety of options, from two-year programs for hopeful grade school teachers to four-year bachelor's degrees in education. In December 1926, Barbe resumed her studies, which now fitted within the home economics curriculum. College-level domestic science and home economic programs had, since their inception, struggled with identity and legitimacy issues. Feminists distrusted the seeming emphasis on the primacy of women's place in the domestic sphere. Academics outside the program often questioned their scholarly integrity and rigorousness, and those within the programs did not always agree on direction. Should home economics programs be considered a "hard" science or a social science or an art? Should they lean toward the academically abstract or the everyday practical?

By the 1920s, many proponents offered a vision that combined all these facets. The programs no longer simply prepared women to teach at the primary or secondary level; now they could enter professions in fields such as dietetics, social work, interior or textile design, and institutional management. But they still could also be seen as a training ground for future wives and mothers. If women were to effectively manage homes that were both functional and aesthetically pleasing (and most people still assumed this was a women's role), then they would be well served to understand the scientific, technical, social, and historical underpinnings of all facets of that management. So, for example, students combined the abstract with the practical and learned the science (chemistry and biology) and art (presentation) of food selection and preparation. Barbe's classes seemed to offer that balanced approach. Over a span of eighteen months, she took the following courses: Physiology, Commercial Geography, Textile Science, Home Nursing, Rhetoric, and Costume Design.

Unlike her last foray into college, it proved impossible to ignore her other household responsibilities. Stress mounted as other duties vied for her attention. To potentially make matters worse, midway through her return to school her father fell ill and died. But typical of their emotionally estranged relationship, she seemed less distressed about her father's death than the hassles of her life. And those everyday challenges continued unabated. Duncan's respiratory issues continued, sometimes requiring three or four chlorine treatments per day and often waking both of them several times a night. Four sets of renters came and went, one by forced eviction. The house had to be reroofed, obliging her to contend with quotes and workers again. She struggled each month to make her corsetiere quotas. The Woman's Club installed her as historian, and she continued to try to maintain her involvement with the Alliance and the A Volonte Club. Nevertheless, despite all these other pulls on her time, she also immersed herself as much as possible in school life, including taking part in the October 1927 homecoming parade. She and her fellow Home Economic Club members earned a third-place prize for their style showcase of historical clothes commemorating the school's seventieth anniversary. A photo from that parade shows Barbe dressed in costume, with Duncan marching by her side. She continued to include him in as many activities as possible as she struggled to successfully integrate all the facets of her life.

Only a few months after the parade, Barbe made another choice that further complicated her life. In December 1927, with six months of school still remaining, she submitted an application to the Bloomington School District. She likely had assumed that nothing would materialize before the summer, but on January 14 she got an unexpected offer for a teaching position at Edwards School, beginning in just over a week. Returning to work certainly would have been easier and more socially acceptable if she had waited until she graduated and Duncan entered all-day first grade, so it is unclear why she accepted it. But several factors likely played a part. Prices had continued to steadily rise throughout the 1920s, so finances increasingly were an issue. Her new salary was $1,250 per year ($135 for each of the nine school months), so the money certainly was a draw. It placed her within the average salary range for female grade school teachers both locally and nationally, but it was still $600 less than the lowest-paid man in her school district. Despite this inequity, and the fact that it also was well below the wage earned by most factory workers and only slightly above an entry-level clerk position, it still significantly altered her financial status. Beyond simple money issues, however, her return to school had reignited a desire to claim a role beyond middle-class "mother" and Woman's Club social housekeeper. If she looked at her return to teaching as a way to recapture some of her prior sense of personal identity, then she may have feared missing the opportunity.

This fear would have not have been unfounded. Long before the stock market crash of 1929 symbolically began the Great Depression, symptoms of the already broken economy existed. Bloomington schools' economic woes offer an example. The Bloomington School District received the vast majority of its funding from local property taxes. At this point in 1927, tax revenues were already well into what would be a long slide downward. Between 1925 and 1934, property tax revenue dropped by almost half, as real estate assessments fell. During the same time span, school enrollments rose by 10 percent. The property tax rates were set by state law, and only special community referendums could authorize additional moneys. So in an effort to bridge that gap between less money and more students, two separate 1926 referendums asked voters to authorize increased funding for both school operations and school construction. Both failed to pass by substantial margins. The subsequent lack of funds led the school board to cut or reduce courses and teachers in agriculture, music, art, the domestic arts, and printing. The cuts also meant the elimination of the high school band and the only recently implemented kindergarten program, which was one of the reasons Duncan entered kindergarten at ISNU's Metcalf School instead of his local public school. Given the tightened school budget, whether Barbe's decision to take the Edwards teaching position was financial or personal or both, it was likely a smart one.

Regardless of the underlying reason, beginning a new job while still in school meant a stressful six months. She juggled her final classes, her sales job, an attempt to evict a set of renters, the housework, home maintenance, her return to full-time teaching, and Duncan's schedule. She dropped him at school in the morning, but for the first time since his birth she was forced to pay someone to watch him in the afternoon and sometimes in the evenings. Still she avoided the day nursery and instead found a willing neighbor. Those six months were challenging and exhausting but ultimately worth it when on June 7, 1928, she graduated with her diploma in home economics, noting to herself after the ceremony, "John would have been proud."[7] A few weeks after the ceremony, she and Duncan celebrated by taking her newly acquired five-passenger 1925 Moon roadster—complete with a six-cylinder engine and Lockheed hydraulic breaks—on a six-week driving vacation that took them all the way into Maine. Upon their return in late August, they both began what seemed to be a less complicated school year, unaware that the Great Depression loomed on the horizon.

7

Union Organizing and Local Politics, 1929–1937

The October 1929 stock market crash did not cause the economic descent into the Great Depression, but it did accelerate the fall. In the wake of the crash, business and consumer confidence dived, investments dropped, businesses downsized or shut their doors completely, and banks failed. Things worsened over the next two years, and by 1932 the economy had reached rock bottom. The unemployment rate hit 25 percent, and the nation's gross national product was cut in half. The economic free fall affected everyone to some degree. Yet Great Depression hardships hit some harder than others, in part, because the prosperity of the 1920s had also been unevenly distributed. One year before the crash, an estimated 40 percent of Americans already lived in poverty, while the wealth of the top 5 percent exceeded that of the bottom 60 percent. The crash left those already at the bottom with nowhere to turn. As conditions worsened, hundreds of thousands of desperate, unemployed, and often homeless people populated breadlines and lived in temporary shanty towns in parks and vacant lots. Meanwhile, the top 5 percent lost investments and stocks and businesses and, no doubt, also suffered some emotional despair, but rarely did they have to resort to breadlines. Barbe's Great Depression experience fell between those two extremes. Like many middle-class families, she avoided the desperation of the breadline, but she would struggle to make ends meet. In 1928, however, she and Duncan returned from her celebratory graduation trip looking toward a bright future.

They both started back to school in September 1928, and life took on a busy but consistent rhythm. Over the next year, she balanced motherhood, teaching, corset sales, housework, renters, and social commitments while enjoying the first sense of financial stability in nearly five years. Regrettably, that feeling was short-lived. Only one day after the October 1929 crash, she received a telegram announcing a bond company's default. At least eight more default notices followed in the next fifteen months as well as disappointing news regarding drastically reduced or eliminated dividends and payouts on investments not in default. Clearly, her future safety net was shrinking, but its very existence separated her from those on the bottom with no savings or equity. Still other economic blows followed. In November 1931, Berger Brothers stopped taking corset orders, and although Spencer was still in operation, clients were slow to purchase and even slower to pay. She lowered the apartment's rent to twelve dollars per month (from the previous high of forty), but she still struggled to find renters, and more than once tenants disappeared while owing money. Nevertheless, she had a home, and unlike a growing number of people she retained her job. Plus, rapidly dropping prices meant her salary, albeit still low, actually offered more buying power in 1931 than it had in 1929.

This enabled her to lend money to her brother as well as several, already desperate, friends. But she also used her extra funds to have the house painted, buy additional life insurance, take summer camping trips to Colorado and Mackinac Island in 1930 and 1931, trade her car in for a newer-model Chevrolet, and pay for Duncan's fiddlette lessons. (A fiddlette was an inexpensive violin-like instrument sold almost exclusively in Illinois and Wisconsin during the early 1930s.) These expenditures sometimes required dipping into her rapidly depleting savings, but she still had reserves as well as her steady monthly salary, at least for nine months out of the year. She was lucky to have returned to teaching when she did. By 1931 a significant majority of school districts would not hire married women or women with small children. Plus, in general, older women endured higher unemployment rates during the 1930s. A 1931 American Woman's Association study found that 10 percent of women who (like Barbe) had earned between one and two thousand dollars in 1929 found themselves without a job in 1931. Between 1929 and 1931, 25 percent of all working women saw their earnings drop. Having a job with a perceived steady income had led her to believe she was in a somewhat secure position. But as her safety net continued to shrink and the economy did not turn around, funds became less available. For example, she was unable to purchase all twenty-four items on Duncan's September 1931 school list because money ran short. The remaining supplies had to wait until she received her first paycheck at the end of the month. Plus, unbeknownst to Barbe, the security of that paycheck was about to be challenged as the Depression hit Bloomington schools at full force.

As a mother, financial shortfalls had not forced a delay in buying some of Duncan's school supplies until 1931, but as a teacher she had watched a number of students experience this hardship (and worse) for almost two years. Finally, in January 1932, things looked so bad that the "Unemployed Council of Bloomington, Illinois, and Vicinity" stepped in. They demanded that the school board provide free hot lunches and textbooks for the children of the unemployed. Their efforts failed, but the specter of hungry students proved to be just the beginning of the school crisis. The 1926 losing tax referendum, continued population growth, falling real estate tax revenue, and the construction cost of a much-needed new school had left the Bloomington School District's Educational Fund deep in the red. By early 1932, this fiscal hole was so deep the school board declared that unless some solution was found, the Bloomington schools would be shuttered at the end of April. The board first attempted to place the weight of the accommodations solely on the backs of teachers, with a request that teachers volunteer to work the month of May for no pay. Not surprisingly, teachers responded unenthusiastically, so the board turned to the community for help. A special election was scheduled for March 7, 1932, to give citizens the opportunity to approve a property tax rate hike for the purpose of school revenue. Again, not surprisingly given the hard times, this proposed measure proved contentious.

The most organized and aggressive opposition to this tax proposal came from a group known as the Taxpayers Protection League. By 1932 thousands of widely scattered independent organizations, like this one, existed nationwide. Although autonomous, these groups were uniform in their demands for smaller government and reduced taxes. Local agro-businessman Frank H. Funk (former Progressive candidate for governor and recent three-term Republican state senator) aggressively articulated their position. According to Funk, school board mismanagement and overspending had produced the schools' problems, and taxpayers should not be held responsible for the solution. Instead, the tax league claimed the crisis could be averted with significant spending reductions. Cutting teachers' (already low) salaries topped their list. After weeks of concerted effort on their part, the tax league won the day when the rate hike failed by just 80 votes out of the 8,006 cast. Plus, to make matters worse, an early-morning fire destroyed Jefferson School. The fire worsened the school board's overcrowding and fiscal crisis, but it was more personal for Barbe. Jefferson had been her first school as both a Bloomington student and a teacher. No wonder the morning found Barbe feeling "blue and discouraged." Unfortunately, things were not at their worst. The next week, the board talked of paying teachers in "scrip" (a form of credit redeemable for cash at a local bank) and again floated the idea of teachers donating a month of work. The local courts ruled the scrip plan illegal, and teachers continued to resist working for no pay. On March 25, with no solution in sight, Barbe woke to the headline "Money Gone: Teachers and Other Employees Face Payless Payday."[1]

Barbe read this article with dread. She learned that she would receive no paycheck for the month of March and that schools would close on the first of April. This deadline was a full month before previously threatened and only days away. Further, if the proposed tax hike (which the board had managed to schedule for a revote on April 11, 1932) failed, the schools would remain closed until at least September. Teachers struggled with how they should respond to this news, especially in light of a growing community assumption that teachers would, and more important should, place the needs of schoolchildren before their own and stay in class without pay. This societal attitude, which defined female teachers as "natural" nurturers and temporary mother figures rather than professionals, was remarkably enduring. The day before the scheduled school closing, rumors flew, and the teachers discussed possible responses to this growing pressure before being summoned to a mandatory meeting. Once there the superintendent of schools addressed the crisis by supporting the board's no-pay proposal. He argued that voters might take a more favorable view of proposed tax raises if teachers volunteered to sacrifice their salaries. (No mention was made of sacrifice by the higher-paid administrators.) Given the looming reality of closed schools and lack of any real power to say no, "volunteer" is a stretch. Societal assumption aside, they were totally at the whim of the board for their jobs, even in good times. With the threat of a shuttered school and the first failed referendum fresh in their minds, they felt they had little choice. So following this meeting, the school board publicly announced that grade school teachers had declared themselves willing to forego half of their May check and high school teachers 75 percent of their considerably larger salaries if the tax bill passed. Their promised future sacrifice, however, could not solve the immediate crisis, and on the first of April the schools shut their doors and 187 people went unpaid.

These closed doors prompted proponents of the second attempt at a tax levy, including Barbe, to be much more proactive in their efforts to publicize the need for a yes vote. Support came from groups as disparate as the Unemployed Council, the Kiwanis Club, the Business and Professional Women's Club, and the Parent-Teacher Association. In its endorsement of the tax levy, the local newspaper lambasted the Taxpayers Protection League in general and Frank H. Funk in particular. The newspaper slammed their unwillingness to compromise or offer constructive criticism, despite the fact that the teachers and the board had met many of the league's expense-reduction demands. The league remained unmoved by the criticism, and their aggressive campaign against the tax levy continued. And in the end, the teachers' very real present-day (and promised future) sacrifices failed to sway sufficient voters. After a long election day spent electioneering and driving women to the polls, Barbe learned that the tax league had once again proved victorious. More than 12,000 votes were cast, but in the end 153 votes decided the outcome. There would be no tax levy. The board needed to find another solution.

The school board's decisions over the next few months illustrate not only the depth of the fiscal disaster but also the very real lack of power available to school employees, especially classroom teachers. One week after the failed vote, Barbe learned—again from the newspaper, not her employer—that the board had come up with a plan to reopen schools. Teachers would not be paid at all for the time the schools were closed, would give up the previously proposed percentages of their future May checks, and would be paid in "due bills" (basically IOUs) for their unpaid March salaries and remaining contracts. A few board members had stood up for the teachers, arguing that this plan placed the board in breach of its contracts. They failed to sway the majority, but this acrimony helped set the stage for the contested board elections on the horizon. For teachers, little room existed for argument; realistically, either they returned under these conditions or they lost their jobs. Theoretically, Barbe could have stayed home and filed a breached-contract lawsuit, but that was a very risky proposition. Among other things, a lack of tenure protection meant no legal expectation of a future job. The board (re)hired teachers each year on nine-month contracts. So refusing to return this year quite possibly meant no rehire the following year. For most teachers, including Barbe, that risk outweighed a possible future remedy of recouping three months of lost salary on a current contract. It also would have done nothing to counter the present-day economic realities. So the schools reopened, and all the teachers returned under these new conditions. Unfortunately, these measures did not solve the economic crisis, and at the end of the month the board cut an additional $70,000 from its budget by slashing both staff and salaries. Now everyone from the superintendent to the school janitors saw their salaries reduced, and a number of physical educators, school nurses, music supervisors, and grade school teachers were released from their contracts.

Barbe kept her position but with a 10 percent salary reduction that lowered her pay to $1,093.50 per year. Two weeks after this news, she lost another set of renters, further reducing her monthly income. Then two weeks after school ended, she got word of another bond default. In the space of only a few months, Barbe's assumption of continued financial stability had all but disappeared. Luckily, two local grocery stores agreed to take Barbe's "due bills" so she could use them for staples, but due bills could not be used to pay Duncan's added medical expenses. After Barbe and Duncan's trip to Kansas City over the summer to visit a specialist for a weeklong series of tests, doctors placed Duncan on a new (and cutting-edge) adrenaline therapy for his asthma and allergies. The cost was $300 to be paid over two years, plus the expense of required follow-up visits and medicines. Barbe was already struggling, so when classes resumed in September she was disheartened to learn she faced another 10 percent salary reduction, which dropped her monthly income to only $108, or $972 per year. Plus, continuing a practice instituted the previous year, she again had to teach a combined-grade class numbering forty-seven students, many with no books. She tried to keep her situation in perspective. Upon learning that a friend was forced to travel sixteen miles from her home to do housework for another family, Barbe lamented that she "must be desperate for money." She knew she was lucky compared to many, but she still struggled to meet monthly obligations. Plus, every time she learned that yet another bond had defaulted, her "heartbreak" over her financial future grew.[2]

While Barbe personally struggled, efforts to solve the school budget issue continued. A partial (and temporary) solution was reached when the state legislature authorized (for the first time) a referendum vote for a onetime bond sale to be used for school operating funds. The board bartered a shaky agreement with the citizen-led tax league, and the latter dropped their public fight against the plan. The November 8, 1932, vote illustrated both a local and a national call for change. Bloomington voted Democratic for the first time in decades, helping to elect Franklin D. Roosevelt as president and overwhelmingly pass the $125,000 bond issue. Only a few weeks later, this new revenue source allowed for $65,000 worth of "due bills" to be redeemed for cash. Barbe celebrated the influx. "Lived in style today—setting a respectable looking table in dining room."[3] Unfortunately, these funds proved to be only a temporary patch, and less than two years later the schools once again were in danger. And in some ways, the process simply repeated itself. The school board once again turned to the voters to ask for a tax hike to partially offset the lower revenues stemming from reduced property values. The tax league once again argued aggressively against it. And once again, the March 1934 vote was very close. But this time, the outcome was different. By a margin of only twenty-one votes, Bloomington approved the permanent real estate tax hike. This victory was, in part, the result of other changes also unfolding between 1932 and 1934.

During these same two years, the composition of local governing units changed as well. Bloomington (like most voters) had supported Roosevelt in the 1932 election, but uncharacteristically the community also continued to vote Democrats into some local offices. In 1933 Democrats gained the mayor's office and several city council seats and then added two more seats in 1934, bringing the distribution nearly even with seven Republicans and six Democrats. The school board also saw a shift. In 1932 an active unionist and printer with no experience in public affairs defeated an incumbent for a seat on the board. This victory signaled (according to a *Pantagraph* editorial) the community's wish for new leadership. The following year, another newcomer, M. L. Hauser, a Bloomington Trades and Labor Assembly (BTLA) union organizer and leader, decisively won a seat on the school board. Then in 1934, a plumber also active in the BTLA defeated the then current school board president, ending his eighteen years of service. The school board was still dominated by attorneys and businessmen who leaned toward cutting school expenditures (and teacher salaries) as a necessary component to all budget options; nevertheless, the election of these three men was part of a wider bump for local Democratic union-supporting candidates. This shift turned out to be relatively short-lived for the community at large, but not Barbe. Her role as a charter member of a recently organized local Democratic women's group provided the context for much of her political support in the decades to come. In the immediate period, however, the changing school board helped instigate a dramatic shift in her path.

When the 1933–1934 school year began, Barbe's circumstances remained challenging. Her pay still was only $108 per month, and the precarious education fund meant her job itself stood on shaky ground. She was not alone. By the spring of 1933, nationwide 330,000 children and almost 50,000 teachers had been sent home by school closures. Chicago schoolteachers had already faced a school year in which they received only three months' pay. Throughout the country, teachers who retained their jobs or returned after layoffs almost always faced reduced salaries and often larger classes, shorter school terms, and insufficient supplies. Solutions were unsure and slow to come. The National Education Association, to which Barbe's ISTA was an affiliate, was slow and cautious in its response. As a whole, the NEA was a "top-down" organization vested in promoting higher standards of professionalization and maintaining the hierarchical educational structure. Its initial response to the crisis centered on research and reports that proved informative but largely ineffective in actually mitigating reality. For example, a series of studies concluded current local real estate tax rates had proved to be an inadequate and highly inequitable way to fund schools. At the same time, however, the NEA and its state and local affiliates also strove not to alienate the business community, which meant no wholesale support for tax increases. As a whole, the NEA and its affiliates remained focused on the creation of a cabinet-level secretary of education while also pushing for state- and federal-level educational funding reform. During the fall and winter of 1933–1934, the ISTA concentrated their efforts on reform in Illinois.

Throughout Illinois schools continued to be at risk of closure due to lack of funds. In December 1933, after prompting from the ISTA legislative committee, the state superintendent of schools asked newly elected Democratic governor Henry Horner for emergency school relief legislation. As a result, during the same early months of 1934 that Bloomington argued (for the third time in three years) over a proposed (and this time ultimately successful) local tax levy, the Illinois General Assembly and the governor wrangled over efforts to find emergency relief for schools from the state's already depleted coffers.

Some saw the answer in revenues from the pending Liquor Control Act necessitated by the repeal of the Eighteenth Amendment in December 1933. Others supported gas taxes, while others lobbied for income taxes or sales taxes or taxes on grain futures. No consensus could be reached. For months the local newspaper reported on the state-level legislative gridlock and rancor alongside another front-page story, the manhunt for the infamous gangster John Dillinger. By the time law enforcement gunned down Dillinger in front of a Chicago theater in July 1934, multiple tax measures had failed. Ultimately, the governor would divert one-third of the state motor fuel tax to education, but in those early months of 1934 Barbe had reason to feel hopeless.

Barbe's involvement with the ISTA stretched back to her earliest days of teaching, and she took part in its early 1934 legislative lobbying effort, sending telegrams and phoning congressmen. But it seemed to accomplish very little. Plus, as the local March 1934 tax levy date approached and the state seemed no closer to a solution to the educational crisis, the ISTA seemed detached from the immediate nature of the crisis. For example, the Central Division brought 1,200 teachers to Bloomington in the first week of March 1934 for the local affiliate's annual meeting. The board closed schools so the teachers could attend, and Barbe heard speakers celebrate new trends in education such as the limits of "book learning" and the uses of functional philosophy. As a delegate to the three-day state-level ISTA annual meeting in 1934, she took part in sessions in which ideas about increasing the long-term fiscal health of education took center stage. Although both events addressed important issues, neither offered immediate solutions for her current problems; instead, they primarily offered a macro approach to educational issues. And while that broad strategy offered possible long-term ameliorative solutions, Barbe's day-to-day struggles were immediate. Plus, in the conservative top-down structure of the NEA, the Central Division of the ISTA was a very small cog in a very large machine. Looking for more immediate and local solutions led Barbe to consider a long-ignored path of possible change: unions.

Teachers' unions were not a new phenomenon. Chicago teachers had led the way during the Progressive Era, as growing numbers of (mostly urban) teachers across the country organized. In 1916 this independent grassroots effort looked to strengthen their mission by bringing their numbers together, and the Chicago Teachers Federation became Local 1 of the newly formed American Federation of Teachers. The new union quickly affiliated with the AFL and within four years boasted more than 170 locals and a membership of 9,000. But that successful growth proved to be short-lived. Soon after the AFT affiliated with the AFL, the Chicago School Board prohibited teachers from belonging to any organization affiliated with trade unionism. As a result, the Chicago teachers were forced to pull out of the AFT. Things worsened in the 1920s, as the idea spread that union activity was an un-American and unnecessary goal in the expanding capitalist marketplace. This antiunion, probusiness climate drastically reduced union numbers even further. By 1926 AFT membership had fallen to only about 3,000, and by 1929 only 39 AFT locals still existed. In comparison, the NEA, which flourished in the conservative atmosphere of the 1920s, grew to more than 220,000 members by 1931. The AFT's struggle for survival echoed the challenges faced by unions nationwide, but women's organizations were hit particularly hard. Of the approximately 11 million working women in the United States, only 250,000 (less than 3 percent) were unionized in 1930, and half of those members came from the ranks of the garment workers. Even Barbe, who was part of a union household, had failed to show any inclination toward unions as an avenue of change. But all of that was about to change. In 1930 the future of organized labor looked bleak, but as the times turned even bleaker Barbe, like a growing number of people, considered the merits of change from below rather than above.

Before this crisis, the ISTA (as an affiliate of the NEA) seemed to serve as an adequate professional support organization. But the Depression had brought Barbe's preexisting powerlessness as a teacher to the forefront. She was coming to realize that although the ISTA still could play a role, its efforts to not alienate the business class or weaken administrative dominance did little to counter her present situation. Contrary to that approach, the AFT aggressively fought for classroom teachers' rights, or, more accurately, against their lack of rights. Barbe, like many teachers throughout the nation, had no tenure status, no guarantee of a contract from year to year, no means of salary negotiation, and only limited pension benefits. The school board controlled the entire process. She often did not receive a contract offer for the September start date until summer, and she had no control over where she taught or what grade she taught or how many students she taught. By 1933 Barbe had already been moved to a combined- and lower-grade classroom against her wishes and had her request for a position at a school closer to her home denied. She also wanted an opportunity to put her diploma to use and teach or supervise home economics, but that request also failed to be granted. The NEA and its affiliates did not offer solutions for these challenges, so when school board member and BTLA organizer M. L. Hauser approached Barbe in late 1933 to discuss possible interest in helping to organize local teachers, she said yes.

The BTLA traced its history back to 1891, when local trade unions came together to form a unified voice. The group, first affiliated with the radical Knights of Labor and then after 1902 with the more conservative AFL, endorsed political candidates, supported strikers, and helped organize new locals. J. B. had been an active member and leader of the BTLA from the time he arrived in Bloomington until his death. In the decade after J. B. passed, the 1920s antiunion efforts had weakened their numbers and strength, but the economic downturn of the Depression offered a context for their revival. Attesting to their ability to work with more conservative factions, the BTLA, along with local clergy, the American Legion, and the Association of Commerce and Industry, formed the Civic Relief Committee, which focused on finding work for the unemployed. But they also organized the aforementioned Unemployed Council. The council promoted class solidarity and offered weekly forums where people could discuss the possibilities of more radical, and often anticapitalistic, solutions to the crisis. More pragmatically, in addition to pushing for lunches and textbooks for students, they also lobbied for lower power bills, rent relief, and unemployment insurance for the more than 2,000 out-of-work Bloomington residents and their families. By 1933, however, the BTLA had returned to its central purpose thanks to New Deal legislation. In 1933 federal legislators reversed their post–World War I antiunion stance and recognized workers' rights to organize. Then in 1935, they strengthened this right with the passage of the National Labor Relations Act (commonly known as the Wagner Act), which added penalties for private employers that refused to recognize unions. This legislation helped create a context in which the BTLA could turn its attention to the previously stalled effort at organizing unions.

In 1932 federal legislators also removed one of the blocks educators faced when they outlawed the "yellow-dog contracts" used to force teachers to promise not to join a union. But, unfortunately, the Wagner Act would not extend the guarantee of union rights or recognition to public-sector employees (for example, public school teachers). Despite this lack, teachers increasingly looked to unions for help, and the AFT aggressively looked to grow their depleted numbers. Locally, the BTLA included teachers in their organizing efforts, and the group played an instrumental role in the birth of Bloomington's first teachers' union. Luckily for the AFT, labor councils throughout the nation demonstrated this same level of solidarity. The AFT's national growth relied on their recruiting help and continued support, as they simply did not have sufficient staff to do it all themselves. Bloomington certainly followed this pattern. Hauser met with Barbe in the late fall of 1933 to discuss union possibilities, and then the BTLA issued an invitation to a formal organizing meeting on behalf of the AFT. On January 9, 1934, 35 teachers answered this call, and that night 20 people (including Barbe) signed a pledge card. Duncan was now nearly thirteen years old, and his maturity allowed her the flexibility to commit fully to this effort, and things moved quickly in the following days. By February 6, the initial converts felt confident enough to form a nominating committee, with Barbe as its vice president, as well as a Constitution Committee, on which she also served. The latter group worked on the constitution almost every night for a week, while also trying to recruit new members, before convening another meeting on February 14, 1934. By the end of that evening, just over 60 teachers had approved the constitution; chosen executive officers, including Barbe as the federation's vice president; and officially become American Federation of Teachers Local 276: the Bloomington Federation of Teachers (BFT).

In the weeks that followed, other teachers followed their lead, and soon their numbers topped 150. By early March, the new union boasted the membership of a vast majority of local teachers. As BFT members, they also became part of a larger network of labor organizations that included not only the AFT and the BTLA but also the Illinois Federation of Labor (IFL) and the AFL. But even given all this support, in reality the BFT still had little real power. As their organizational objectives note, they counted on "mutual assistance and cooperation . . . with the parent-teacher association, the board of education and such officials in matters of mutual concern."[4] Soon after their inception, Barbe was tasked with meeting IFL president Reuben Soderstrom, and no doubt he offered advice on negotiations and strategies. Unfortunately, the school board had no legal obligation to recognize or bargain with the union. Nevertheless, for Barbe and no doubt many of the others, the advent of "our teacher federation" (as she often called it) offered a proactive way to combat feelings of powerlessness not necessarily provided by other support systems. Contrary to the ISTA's and NEA's long-term approach, only days after its formation the BFT took a small step toward an immediate goal. They requested that the school board issue their contracts in April rather than waiting until the summer. Their next step was a riskier one. During the first week of March 1934 (at the same time the ISTA–Central Division annual meeting offered discussions of functional philosophy), the BFT issued a bold statement. If the upcoming tax levy vote fell short again and the state continued to offer no solution, then the Bloomington schools would have to close. In short, they declared themselves to be professionals, not volunteers, who would be paid their full salaries in cash—no more scrip or IOUs or promises of future pay. Then they went to work to gain support for their agenda.

Locally, they lobbied loudly for the passage of the tax levy and against the Taxpayers Protection League. At the state level, they lobbied their congressmen and governor in support of statewide school relief. The state continued to be deadlocked, but thanks in part to their hard work they achieved success locally with the passage (by twenty-one votes) of the March 1934 tax increase. But even with the added funds, the board announced plans to slash the 1934–1935 operating budget by another ten thousand dollars. These cuts were to come mostly in the form of salaries, library operations, and indigent-student aid. This news added import to the BFT's new goal of electing another prolabor member to the school board. Barbe, along with other BFT and BTLA members, aggressively electioneered, and in April 1934 they successfully unseated the board president by electing the BTLA-backed candidate. This addition seemed to bode well for cooperation between the board and the BFT. Barbe, in particular, continued to play a central role. Only days after the election, school board member and BTLA representative M. L. Hauser sought Barbe out to discuss the superintendent's plan to remove two teachers. One of those teachers had chosen to fight her removal, claiming that it stemmed from a personal, not professional, clash with the superintendent. A committee including Barbe, the BFT president, and Hauser met with all the parties and averted her firing. This sense of empowerment continued. In late April, the board issued contracts for the following year. The BFT's Executive Board also began to consider the merits of instigating a "cadet" (student) teaching program to help overworked teachers. Unfortunately, in the midst of these professional victories, Barbe suffered a personal loss.

In May 1934, her mother suffered a heart attack and died only three days later. This death hit her much harder than her father's had, but responsibility left little time for mourning. She spent only a day in Odell for the funeral before returning home. The school year ended soon after this tragedy, bringing the usual summer work of intense housecleaning and repairs along with gardening, canning, and other warm-weather tasks. But this summer, she added BTLA work to that list. In particular, she worked on arranging the roster for the union supporters' biggest celebration, Labor Day, choosing John H. Walker as the principal speaker. Walker boasted impressive labor credentials as a former president of the Illinois Mine Workers followed by the presidency of the Illinois Federation of Labor and an eventual run for governor on the 1920 Farm-Labor ticket (on which J. B. had also run as treasurer). In 1930 a power struggle within the mine workers' union had led to the end of his tenure in the IFL, but by 1934 he represented the Illinois Men's Teachers Union. His appearance was a successful component of a day marred by rain cancellations, and Barbe proudly stood by his side on the Coliseum stage as the Labor Day contingent honored J. B. Lennon's service to labor nearly twelve years after his death.

But that summer of 1934 had also offered a respite from some of the tensions of work and school and union duties. Like millions of other Americans looking for a diversion from the hard times, Barbe and Duncan managed to find a few days to visit the Chicago's World's Fair. Like its 1893 "Columbian Exhibition" predecessor, the 1933–1934 "Century of Progress" fair was wildly successful. While the 1893 version gave the world the first Ferris wheel and impressed visitors with the architectural beauty of the "White City," this fair dazzled with a "Rainbow City" of different-colored buildings lit by neon lights and offered its own crowd-drawing attraction. The Sky Ride suspended riders 200 feet in the air as rocket-shaped cars sped 2,000 feet along a steel wire suspended between two 628-foot steel towers. The entire fair and much of the city could also be viewed from the observation decks topping the towers, which were the tallest structures in Chicago at this time. If all of that was too much, then a multitude of ground-level exhibits celebrated the technological advances of the industrial age from "dream cars" to Wonder Bread's innovations in bread baking. The two had managed to visit the fair for a few days the prior summer as well, and both enjoyed the spectacle again. But for Duncan, another event may have topped the fair. He was such an avid Chicago Cubs fan that Barbe had allowed him to miss school two years prior so he could listen to the radio broadcast of the 1932 World Series. Sadly, the Cubs had lost that series in four games to the New York Yankees, but on this trip he got to watch them defeat their archrivals, the St. Louis Cardinals, live at Wrigley Field.

The Chicago trip offered a short respite from the challenges she continued to face as the head of her household. Her budget still suffered from the effects of her reduced (and sometimes nonexistent) salary, plus she also had to contend with slow corset sales, continued investment losses, and another set of renters moving out. But despite the testing times, as the 1934–1935 school term began, potential seemed to be on the horizon. She had finally been transferred to a school closer to home, the newly rebuilt Jefferson. The board had also promised a 5 percent raise to teachers for the following (1935–1936) school year. Duncan was thriving. Like his mother in years past, he became the editor of his school's newspaper on top of his involvement in many activities, including the Boy Scouts and DeMolay (the Masonic affiliate for young men). He also worked at his first jobs, delivering newspapers and selling magazines. In 1935, after his eighth grade graduation, he continued to excel as a student at ISNU's highly regarded high school. His asthma continued to be a problem, but he had also begun to administer his own adrenaline shots. His maturity and independence gave Barbe not only the flexibility to join the union fight but also the space to return to her own studies. She investigated what it would take to turn her home economics three-year diploma into a four-year bachelor's degree. The path seemed feasible, so in February 1935 she once again found herself in an ISNU extension class. She would continue to pursue that degree goal periodically over the next decade.

She also continued her union work. Much like J. B. in his time, she became an increasingly active member of the BTLA. Not long after the birth of the BFT, the BTLA's chief organizer asked her to speak to other groups as a union recruiter. Long-held apprehension about public speaking made her hesitant, but as the group was small she reluctantly agreed. This first effort earned her congratulations at the subsequent BTLA meeting, when, as proudly noted by Barbe, "[he] lauded me to the skies for helping him to organize the Beauty Operators." As the BFT's elected delegate to the BTLA, Barbe continued to help them in organizing efforts as they reached out to the "oil men" and store clerks. In January 1935, she also was elected to the BTLA Board of Trustees (that is, the Executive Board). The accolades continued when in February 1935, she had the honor of sitting at the speaker's table with AFT president Raymond Lowry when he spoke at the

BFT's first annual banquet. But not all looked clear on the horizon. Only weeks after the BFT's first anniversary, both the BFT and the BTLA held special meetings in anticipation of the coming local election season. They had reason to worry. New Deal Democrats tended to support the union movement, but the local tide seemed to be turning back toward the Republicans. Plus, much of the BFT's success had come from their working relationship with the school board, and, in Barbe's words, "a desperate effort is being made to defeat our present [School] Board."[5]

News reports back her assessment. Eight candidates sought the three open three-year seats, and, for the first time ever, candidates grouped themselves into factions. The campaign and public debate were, as described by the local newspaper, "spirited." The group backed by the BFT and the BTLA included the current board president, Kaywin Kennedy, and BTLA member James Griggs. The opposing faction included two potential new members and current board member Roy Ramseyer. The campaigning revealed tensions between the current board members as well as varying degrees of support for the promised 5 percent raise for teachers. None of the candidates claimed to be against the modest bump, which was quite small compared to the more than 20 percent cuts teachers had taken in 1932 (and still endured). But while Kennedy and Griggs offered wholesale support, Ramseyer's words were measured. He noted that raises were "desirable" but only "as the board's revenues allow."[6] Numerous local offices were also contested, with Republican candidates hoping to retake their former dominance. For weeks Barbe distributed election information and canvassed for votes. On election day, she worked before school and during her lunch to get the Democratic vote out. Unfortunately, the work was for naught. In the largest-ever turnout for a school board election, both Kennedy and Griggs lost, as Ramseyer and his faction took the three open seats. The Democrats were also soundly defeated. They retained only the mayor's seat, as they lost ground on the city council and in almost every other contest.

In the days after the election loss, the BTLA officially thanked Barbe for her extensive help, but she was still disheartened and exhausted by this turn of events, which disappointed on two levels. She believed in the cause, but she also believed a win would have meant a possible position as principal. Unfortunately, more bad news followed. The week after the election, the new school board president, Ramseyer, delivered the blow at a special federation meeting. There would be no 5 percent raise. The election loss followed by the salary news seemed to take some of the spirit from the local union. Barbe attended the next (and last for the school year) meeting, but it failed to even turn out enough members for a quorum. Nevertheless, this downturn did not signify the end. A core group of (mostly female) BFT members, including Barbe, continued their efforts. Unfortunately, the Depression years never gave them another school board as receptive to their influence as the 1934–1935 board roster.

In the wake of the unfortunate 1935 election results, Barbe also stayed committed to the BTLA. In an era in which a majority of citizens believed women needed to step aside to allow men to take the lead, the BTLA and the BFT displayed a very progressive attitude toward gender equity. Both groups offered leadership opportunities for women, and Barbe served at times as a delegate, board member, union organizer, and chair of various committees for both organizations. Her work with the BFT salary committee was especially vital, as the Depression continued with no end in sight. A year after the 1935 salary disappointment, the board finally offered a small 3.4 percent raise. This bump, effective in September 1936, brought Barbe to a still very low twelve hundred dollars per year. Unfortunately, by that time, however, her somewhat dire financial straits had led to a rift between Barbe and the BTLA. In the summer of 1936, she simply did not have the money to hire union workers to paint her badly peeling house, so she gave the work to a nonunion crew. She pleaded her case to the Painters' Union to no avail. They wanted her jettisoned not only from the BTLA but also from the BFT as punishment. After a stress-filled week that left her covered in hives, she chose to resign her various positions with the BTLA so as not to jeopardize the BFT's status in the group. The BFT, however, was not as unyielding as the BTLA, and the vacuum of time created by her sudden BTLA removal quickly filled. She helped to guide through the charter for a BFT-affiliated credit union and served on its board and as the primary loan investigative officer. She also continued as Jefferson School's official BFT delegate, served on committees for numerous local groups, and electioneered (mostly unsuccessfully) for local school board candidates sympathetic to teachers' issues. In addition to these local efforts, she also participated in organizing the Illinois Federation of Teachers (IFT) in 1937. This state-level work turned out to be only a small part of the next phase of her activism that increasingly found her expanding her efforts beyond the local.

8

From Local Organizer to National Reformer, 1937–1945

Barbe had first stood tentatively in front of a rural McLean County classroom in 1902. Thirty-five years later, the professional educator who strode confidently into her Bloomington classroom bore little resemblance to that deferential "schoolmarm" of 1902. But it was not merely the passing of time that had brought that shift; she had actively pursued change. Her ongoing commitment to higher education and activism stretching back to the Progressive Era built the confidence and skills necessary for her transformation into a professional educator as well as a local union organizer and political lobbyist. Her recent efforts to organize the local teacher federation and shape the Bloomington School Board had sprung from a desire to gain some control over the parameters of her career, which had been badly compromised by economic crisis. As the Depression endured, however, concentrating only on local solutions proved insufficient. As a result, by 1937 she had also begun to turn her gaze outward beyond the local to the state and national arena. During the next eight years, she devoted considerable time and effort to these expanded efforts. The American Federation of Teachers and the Women's Trade Union

League (WTUL) helped lay the groundwork for this broader approach by offering opportunities to ground "bread-and-butter" wage issues in a wider social context. This work also proved to complement her increasingly important Unitarian-based view of the world. The end result was an arc of activism stretching from the 1930s, through World War II, and beyond that was both liberal and pragmatic.

The WTUL was key to this process of putting liberal belief into pragmatic actions. Founded in 1903 (one year after Barbe's high school graduation), the WTUL embodied the radical goal of bringing together working-class and middle-class women to fight for women's labor rights. Like many of Barbe's widening interests, local union affiliations paved the initial path. In this case, she served as the BFT delegate to a WTUL convention in 1935. Her interest in the group remained on the back burner, as she devoted her energies to local battles over the next two years, but by 1937 she was ready to become more involved. In April 1937, acting again as a BFT delegate, Barbe traveled to Chicago for the WTUL annual conference, where she was elected to the Executive Board of the Illinois WTUL. This meeting's primary purpose was to prepare for an upcoming legislative battle. The Illinois General Assembly had finally agreed to seriously consider the women's eight-hour maximum-day bill first introduced by the WTUL more than two decades prior.

The national WTUL is perhaps best known for its Progressive Era participation in some of the most high-profile and contentious strikes of that time. But for more than fifty years, the national and local chapters also devoted energy to the passage of protective labor laws designed to set maximum hours and minimum pay rates for women. Throughout this long fight, they experienced varying degrees of success, depending largely on the social, political, and economic trends of the time. During the Progressive Era, social housekeeping middle-class women attained considerable success in achieving legislative reforms focused on "protecting" working-class women. The courts proved supportive as well. In 1908 the Supreme Court's *Muller v. Oregon* decision validated this path by upholding a maximum-hour law for women based on the need to protect their presumed present or future status as mothers.

By the 1920s, the WTUL had lost some of its radical edge and devoted most of its energies to fighting for labor legislation. Unfortunately, after the 1920 suffrage victory, their tack lost momentum as legislators and probusiness courts proved less open to the argument that women needed special protections. The 1923 *Adkins v. Children's Hospital* decision directly cited women's supposed post–Nineteenth Amendment legal equality when they struck down a minimum-wage law for women. But things changed again during the Depression years. Economic crisis and high unemployment lent themselves to the resurgence of traditional views in which women should stay out of the paid workforce. But even traditionalists understood that Depression reality meant some women simply had to work. So once again, support grew for the WTUL argument that society should protect the health (that is, maternal capacities) of those women forced into the wage world. At the same time, proponents also pointed out protecting women's wages and welfare reduced their potential drain on society by minimizing their need for the new forms of relief and government aid. In 1937 protective labor laws saw success again when the Court upheld minimum-wage legislation for women based on both of those ideas.

In 1937 the Illinois legislature joined this trend and prepared to vote on the long-tabled WTUL-backed women's eight-hour maximum-day bill. Specific strategies for its passage took center stage at the Illinois WTUL annual meeting, which also drew support from the national WTUL, the AFL, and various Illinois legislators. In the following months, Barbe, as a WTUL representative, traveled to Springfield numerous times to lobby for this eight-hour-day effort, as did other activists and national WTUL staff. Later that summer, victory was achieved. The general assembly passed and Illinois governor Henry Horner signed the bill. In acknowledgment of her effort, Barbe was among only five hundred people invited to attend the July "Victory Dinner" at the Chicago Woman's Club. She thoroughly enjoyed the chance to mingle with like-minded reformers, including national WTUL leaders Agnes Nestor and Mary Halas. These liberal-minded labor leaders and women's rights supporters shared the assumption that women's equality did not negate the need to provide protections

from exploitation. It was liberalism that clearly incorporated a pragmatic view regarding the needs of working women. Despite Barbe's
focus on the practical applications of laws regarding women's equality, her progressive approach to race relations exhibited a pattern of
thought and behavior that seemed centered less on day-to-day practi-
cality and more on idealism.

The population of McLean County was overwhelmingly white
during the first half of the twentieth century. Despite this fact, Barbe
had not been completely isolated in a "white-only" bubble. ISNU
and the Bloomington public schools had been integrated since the
nineteenth century, and she had both attended school with and
taught classes to black and white students. Over the years, Barbe often made comments about her students in her journals, and although
these notations could be very personal and rather uncomplimentary
they were never racially toned. But it is not just the lack of overt
rhetorical racism that provides evidence of Barbe's progressive racial
attitude. Despite local discrimination and de facto segregation that
marred the entire first half of the twentieth century, Barbe's actions
displayed a decided lack of prejudice. She attended myriad multicultural and integrated events offered by the YWCA and Unitarian
Church, both of which actively promoted the idea of racial equality.
She also took advantage of open invitations from local African American organizations to take part in events over the years that varied
from listening to a black minister speak on Benjamin Banneker to
attending the 1954 celebration marking the renovation of the local
Methodist AME Church. But an even more personal example likely
speaks the loudest.

In 1926 Barbe sold a corset to Julia Duff, an African American
woman in town visiting family. Like Barbe, Duff had attended ISNU
as a home economics student, with Duff leaving in 1915, the year
Barbe arrived. She also was a teacher. After visiting Duff's parents'
house to fit her, Barbe noted in her journal, "At Miss Duff's, a colored
girl in Normal. . . . Is very nice—a teacher in Tulsa."[1] This example
is so telling for several reasons. First, the language (although perhaps
not apparent to modern readers) is extremely respectful for the time.
During the 1920s, the Ku Klux Klan had rapidly risen in acceptance,

popularity, and numbers throughout the nation, and McLean County was no exception. Only a year after Barbe's visit to the Duff's, the Klan held a widely attended parade in Bloomington. In concert with the racial attitude embodied by the Klan, both violent and casual racism had also become increasingly common. So Barbe's use of *colored* (instead of the still all too common *nigger*) and the honorific of *Miss* (instead of the widely accepted use of only first names for African Americans) offers a perfect illustration of her private mind-set. Plus, by this point, segregation in Bloomington had become increasingly common, so her visit to the Duffs' home served as a public show of respect that many whites would have found unacceptable. This essential attitude of respect was a necessary personal foundation for her eventual move toward a greater commitment to legislative racial justice. Her involvement with the AFT added a wider context for this commitment to grow.

Like her connection to the WTUL, Barbe's involvement with her local union had led her to the AFT. Acting as a BFT delegate, Barbe attended several national-level conventions in the late 1930s that offered exposure to the political and economic components of broad social change. Similar to the WTUL, the AFT had also retreated from some of its extreme Progressive Era radical origins, but it remained considerably more progressive than the mainstream on some issues, including the quest for racial equality. For example, throughout the 1930s, the AFT demanded equal salaries for white and black teachers (as they did for men and women). The organization fell short of calling for immediate desegregation in the South, but it did document the significant differences in funding and facilities between the supposed "separate but equal" segregated schools. During this same period, most AFT locals were also integrated, unlike most local divisions of the rival National Education Association. Again, the organization fell short of demanding that the still-segregated southern locals desegregate, but as a whole the AFT attempted to act on its liberal racial ideals. It actively recruited African American members, and in 1934 the national convention moved its entire setup to another hotel after a racial incident. The next year, annual convention delegates elected an African American professor as the AFT's national vice president.

Racial solidarity served as part of the AFT's strategy to grow and strengthen, even as the AFL resisted efforts in that same direction.

As part of its campaign to educate its membership, AFT vice president Mary Herrick visited Bloomington in 1937 and spoke to the local federation about the need for antilynching legislation and laws to address the oppressive effects of sharecropping. Not long after attending that lecture (and only two weeks after the WTUL eight-hour-day victory), Barbe made the trip to the Lorraine Hotel in Madison, Wisconsin, for the AFT annual meeting. After officials remedied a credential mix-up that almost kept her off the floor, she enjoyed speeches by various labor leaders as well as progressive Wisconsin governor Philip La Follette. But the inclusive and liberal tenor of the affair was nearly destroyed by a hotel worker's rude treatment toward a black delegate. In response, hotel restaurant workers (in solidarity with the AFT) threatened a strike, which resulted in a profuse management apology that kept the AFT on site. A year later, Barbe served as a delegate at the 1938 annual meeting in Cincinnati that, like the 1934 convention, chose to move its venue when it became clear that African American delegates were not going to receive equal treatment. Clearly, the AFT's commitment to racial equality was not always a fiscally practical road, but for members like Barbe this path offered a way to demonstrate that liberal ideals could overshadow pragmatism.

Liberal ideals were not always so clearly defined, however, nor did liberalism always trump pragmatism. The 1938 AFT convention offered an internal battle that proved that point. The AFT had served as a longtime affiliate to the AFL. The relationship had not always been a smooth one, however, and the Depression had increased tensions. By 1935 the two unions were at odds over the AFL's failure to show any real support for struggling teachers. It refused to hire new AFT organizers or push more aggressively for teachers' inclusion in the Wagner Act. In short, the AFT felt somewhat abandoned by the AFL leadership. At the same time, teachers were not the only unhappy AFL affiliates. In 1935 the internal AFL Committee for Industrial Organization had requested endorsement for mass industrial-based locals, which contrary to AFL norms organized without regard to skill, gender, or race. This internal petition had failed, and when the recalcitrant committee members refused to back down from their demands, AFL leadership ousted them. By 1938 the Congress of Industrial Organizations (CIO) had established itself as an AFL rival, and the 1938 AFT convention in Cincinnati seemed to offer the liberal teachers' union a chance to make a change in affiliation from the conservative AFL to the CIO.

The choice, however, was not as easy as it seemed. From a pragmatic stance, the AFL affiliation connected the small AFT locals to a large network of state and local trade councils such as the Bloomington Trades and Labor Assembly. To lose those connections could very possibly cripple some of the smaller unions like the BFT. But it was not just small unions that saw advantages. The very large Chicago teachers' union had a long cooperative history with the AFL's Illinois Federation of Labor. Nevertheless, other factors worked against the AFL and for the CIO. Even though some local AFL labor councils (such as the BTLA and the IFL) had shown great support for teachers, the conservative "parent" organization of the AFL had a rather dismal record of support for organizing women and minorities, and it consistently treated teachers' unions as an afterthought. Plus, the CIO had a much more inclusive and liberal mind-set, which would have seemed a better match for the AFT; after all, 1938 conventioneers had chosen to change venues in support of their liberal racial ideals.

But disagreement over a different set of ideals further complicated the AFL-CIO choice. In the early years of the Depression, the Communist Party had experienced rapid national growth, as growing numbers of struggling Americans doubted capitalism could save them. Concurrent to this growth, however, reactionary conservatives rose and aggressively condemned communism as anti-American. By 1938 the latter voices were proving to be the strongest, but the fight was not yet over, and the AFT was forced to contend with this ideological and highly political topic. Some of the more liberal (and mostly New York–based) locals embraced communism as the logical answer to the problems that produced the Depression, some of the more conservative members felt deep aversion to the anticapitalistic tenets of communism, and others simply feared that if the AFT did not speak out against communism, then the increasingly negative public pressure would do further harm to teachers. So although the CIO's inclusive nature seemed a good fit to some, others considered their openness far too radical of a risk, and ultimately this latter view won the battle. Conservatives did fail (at this time) to oust all Communist members, but the AFT stayed affiliated with the AFL.

Barbe's specific thoughts on this controversy are unclear, but she very well may have viewed this political tug-of-war as an unneeded distraction from more pressing issues. At the same time the AFT internally battled over its potential political leanings, the somewhat steady path of economic recovery took a deep dip, and unemployment began to rise again. So, hoping to find real-world solutions, she turned again to the WTUL and attended its October 1938 summit on economic issues. This meeting featured IFL leader Victor Olander; the commissioner of the recently established Unemployment Compensation Agency for the State of Illinois, Dr. Peter Swanish; and former WTUL leader and longtime director of the US Department of Labor's Women's Bureau Mary Anderson. All three focused their energies on the pragmatic issues facing workers affected by the ongoing fiscal crisis, but Anderson's work in particular dovetailed with the WTUL's efforts.

The Women's Bureau had from its 1920 inception striven to set policy and pass national-level protective legislation for working women. Director Mary Anderson's involvement in crafting the recently passed 1938 Fair Labor Standards Act was a qualified victory toward that goal. The law definitely had its weaknesses. Maximum weekly hours were set at forty-four (before overtime wages applied), but with a minimum wage of only 25 cents an hour this translated to less than $575 per year. Plus, it covered only about 20 percent of the national workforce, leaving out domestic and agricultural workers, which were jobs predominantly held by women and minorities. Still, as the first federal legislation designed to define and protect workers' rights, it was a start, and the WTUL fully backed it, while also beginning a lobby to extend its benefits to left-out workers.

Immersion in a conference on labor legislation was an intellectually invigorating experience for Barbe, but this trip was not all work. It also provided the opportunity to catch up with an old acquaintance. Barbe and national WTUL leader Agnes Nestor had known each

other for many years. Their acquaintance may have stretched back to
the AFL conventions Barbe attended with the Lennons when she was
a student and beginning teacher and Nestor attended as the head of
the International Glove Workers Union. Regardless of status, women
conventioneers tended to socialize, so the two likely came into contact
at that time. But they clearly became friendly during the 1909 suffrage
train trip to Springfield. In the years after, they periodically exchanged
letters, but once Barbe actively engaged in WTUL work their earlier
ties strengthened. The day after arriving for this 1938 WTUL meeting, Barbe spent the morning with Nestor and her brother, furthering
their friendly bond. They took a long ride around the lake, visited the
homes in a government housing project, and then toured the old fair-
grounds at Grant Park before having dinner together. The day offered
an enjoyable prelude before the real work began the next day. These
strategy sessions were vital, but Barbe's growing commitment to seeking remedies for all working women did not mean that she neglected
issues closer to home. Throughout 1937 and 1938, she also took on
challenges directly affecting teachers.

In 1937 her work with the Bloomington Teachers Federation
had brought her together with other educators to help organize the
Illinois Federation of Teachers. She also remained involved with the
Illinois Education Association (IEA), as the ISTA was known after
1936, even serving as a delegate to national conventions. The IFT's
priority upon its organization had been to use its strength of numbers
to lobby for teacher tenure protection, but the IEA had also become
increasingly aggressive toward this goal. Depression-era job losses explained this shared focus, as teachers increasingly lost their positions
to the less qualified friends and family of school board members and
local politicians. Barbe served as a state-level delegate to both as they
strategized and fought for this protection, but immediate wage issues
also remained a central concern. As such, she also continued her work
on the legislative and salary committees of her local union, hoping to
influence policy. In reality, most of these efforts—from the national
to the local levels—did little to change actual conditions during this
period. She continued teaching large classes with combined grade levels, little support, and low wages. Plus, as always, required meetings

and paperwork consumed time and energy. Extra unpaid duties such as playground supervision and committees proved exhausting as well. The former was sometimes a physical challenge to her barely five-foot frame, and the latter required not only time but often extensive reading, which became more difficult every year as her eyesight deteriorated. (She had been diagnosed with astigmatism in 1915 and struggled with eye issues her entire adult life.) On top of all these challenges, powerful factions began to exert control over the school curriculum in an attempt to eliminate any possible threat of communism.

The AFT leadership would eventually (in 1941) succeed in their attempts to purge their Communist members. But in the interim, the mere presence of even one suspected AFT Communist meant that conservative organizations, such as the American Legion, felt justified in claiming that leftist teachers were plotting to implant unpatriotic ideas into students' heads. To combat this potential threat, the legion had launched extensive campaigns designed to promote their view of "Americanism" in the schools, and school boards proved easy to sway. As a result, Barbe had to incorporate class work designed to promote specific procapitalism and anticommunism agendas. Students constructed American Legion patriotic posters, conducted legion-approved patriotic exercises, and used textbooks endorsed by the American Legion. The legion also used their considerable membership, funds, and growing political clout to push for laws that demanded teachers take loyalty pledges, affirming they were not Communists. These pledges also required teachers to agree not to teach any subject that could be viewed as antithetical to the established government and capitalistic economic system. This extremely murky definition of so-called acceptable teaching topics clearly compromised the ability to cover many important subjects, while it also threatened academic freedom. Civil liberties groups and some unions had fought these pledges, but by 1935 twenty-two states already required them. Illinois avoided these oaths, thanks largely to the aggressive efforts of Chicago union members, but as Barbe's patriotic classroom components attest that did not mean total avoidance of the political pressure.

Pressure did not come only in the form of politics or her teaching career. She had taken a break from her ISNU schedule, but she continued to try to balance work and increased activism with her home life, while constantly dealing with financial pressures. She had largely given up her corsetiere efforts as not worth the time but continued to battle with the hassles of being a landlord. Its value, however, was also up for debate. At one point, a renter once again slipped away owing rent, but this time the deadbeat also stole eight lights along with eight fuses from the meter box. Money was so tight that in April 1937, she was forced to borrow two hundred dollars from a local bank. Thankfully, Duncan continued to offer numerous reasons for pride. He excelled in high school as well as at a variety of extracurricular activities. In the summer of 1937, he turned sixteen and managed to obtain a full-time job at a venetian-blind factory, making seven dollars per week. Barbe worried that he was too young to work so hard, but he remained on the job for the entire summer. That fall he obtained a job at a local grocery store, working after school, on weekends, and over the few next summers. On Barbe's insistence, he saved most of this income. He did, however, loan her fifty dollars to pay off the two-hundred-dollar loan when her finances remained tight. As a whole, the years between 1937 and 1939 had offered both familiar and unfamiliar challenges, all of which frequently left Barbe feeling, as she so often put it, "dead tired." As the decade moved toward its end, no end to that exhaustion appeared on the horizon.

In the spring of 1939, Duncan's high school graduation loomed, and Barbe took on even more activities. She may have looked to fill the void of Duncan's assumed college departure, but these new endeavors also clearly illustrated the continued influence of both the WTUL's and the AFT's pragmatic liberalism. In March 1939, as part of her responsibilities on the Unitarian Church Forum Board, she brought a speaker to town who gave voice to the political side of pragmatic liberalism. Chicago teacher, union organizer, and AFT Executive Council member Lillian Herstein told the Bloomington audience of about two hundred people that only extended New Deal–style government action, which she called socialistic reforms, would keep the United States from succumbing to the triple threats of communism, Fascism, and Nazism. Herstein's speech, which actively promoted liberalism while aggressively condemning communism, represented the

AFT leadership's strategy to combat the belief in some quarters that the AFT was a haven for Communist sympathizers. Ironically, Chicago union members had led the fight to protect members against loyalty oaths, but now many Chicago-based AFT officers, including Herstein, felt that investigating and removing Communists from AFT membership was necessary to save the union.

Herstein's lecture also applauded free speech and warned of the threat represented by monopolized newspapers that too often simply played the part of cheerleader for reactionary politicians. Despite what could be viewed as a somewhat hypocritical disconnect about political freedoms and speech, Barbe and the audience of teachers and labor supporters reacted enthusiastically to her message. A postlecture private reception at the home of fellow Unitarian, former Illinois state (and first female) senator, and current activist Florence Fifer Bohrer offered the venue for a small group to discuss how they could support the freedom of ideas. Two months later, the McLean County Civil Liberties League (CLL) officially organized as an affiliate of the American Civil Liberties Union (ACLU). The ACLU, like the AFT, had been forced to reevaluate how it framed free-speech issues in the wake of perceived Communist threats. A decade prior, the ACLU had actively supported communism's right to exist, but by 1939 the ACLU was at odds with itself. It continued to defend accused Communists, but at the same time some members were trying to distance the group from charges of being a Communist front. The leadership initially split over this issue but in 1940 officially ejected its Communist members. Like the national ACLU, the local league also seemed to have reconciled the condemnation of communism with free speech. And as an Executive Board member, Barbe proudly helped draft their mission "to defend freedom of speech, press and assemblage and other civil rights guaranteed by the constitutions of the United States and the state of Illinois."[2]

In the spirit of that stated mission, the following month Barbe (again along with several fellow Unitarians) helped to organize and served as one of the founding Executive Board members of another new endeavor, the Bloomington-Normal Forum. The forum brought together the CLL with groups such as the Rotary, BFT, BTLA, and

Layman's Society of the Unitarian Church as well as university professors and eventually the National Association for the Advancement of Colored People. Its purpose was to extend what the Unitarian forum had attempted to do for many years: sponsor a variety of multicultural and multifaith national lecturers. Over the next few years, topics ranged from civil liberties and the war crisis in Europe to government-supported health care and America's race problem. Not all speakers were liberals, but on the whole the series did lean to the left. Both the CLL and the forum offered important avenues for discussions about big ideas, and as an Executive Board member Barbe devoted significant time over the years to finding speakers and selling tickets. But Barbe also believed in action. So in 1939, she also added one more thing to her agenda by bringing together six women to organize a local branch of the WTUL. They believed that they could play a bigger role advocating for issues affecting working women if they did not have to rely solely on the state or national branches. In October 1939, the Bloomington-Normal WTUL was officially chartered, with Barbe on the Executive Board.

This new commitment vied for attention against a list of activities that already demanded significant time. She commonly attended two or three separate organizational meetings each day on top of her teaching schedule, mandatory teacher meetings, housework, and parenting responsibilities. The latter, however, was poised to change as Duncan's high school graduation approached. This June 1939 event brought (an almost unheard of) congratulatory letter from Duncan's half brother, John. But more important, it also signaled what was meant to be a new stage for both mother and son as Duncan headed off to college. In anticipation of his departure and to celebrate his graduation, the two once again set off on a road trip that (like her post-ISNU graduation trip eleven years earlier) took them all the way to Maine. En route home, they detoured to New York City, where John Lennon lived, but despite their recent contact failed to connect with him. Nonetheless, the three-day side trip did give them the opportunity to experience city sights. A show at Radio City Music Hall and a prounion Broadway musical revue called *Pins and Needles* offered high culture, while enjoying a vending-machine lunch mat restaurant supplied a very novel slice of everyday ur-

at an automat restaurant supplied a very novel slice of everyday urban life. Barbe also got a chance to enjoy her still favorite pastime of window-shopping, and she marveled at Macy's and Saks before walking to Greenwich Village to see what the budding artistic center and bohemian neighborhood was like. The highlight of their New York stay, however, may have been the World's Fair.

Like the fairs before it, the "Building the World of Tomorrow"–themed fair required a signature event. The Perisphere and Trylon were meant to be that signature. The Perisphere (a spherical exhibit building suspended over a reflecting pool) connected to a three-sided obelisk (the Trylon) by a custom-made escalator. They were designed to provide a space to marvel at a model of a city of the future. Barbe and Duncan paid twenty-five dollars to experience the "future," but unfortunately fair funds had run a bit short and the event was not quite as tall or polished as the designers had hoped. This may account for Barbe's lack of enthusiasm for the view of supposed utopia. This lackluster response stood in stark contrast to her delight in that evening's entertainment at the Lagoon of Nations. This spectacle combined music, water fountains, lights, and fireworks in a fifteen-minute display of gorgeous synchronicity. Nearly sixty years later, the Las Vegas Bellagio Hotel could offer a similar show every fifteen minutes, but in 1939 the whole event was an innovative and extravagant display that Barbe clearly found a marvel. The next day, the pair headed back to Bloomington, finishing their three-week vacation a week before the new school year was to begin.

Upon their return, Duncan had hoped to enter either Harvard or the University of Illinois. His grades and test scores guaranteed him a spot at both schools, but unfortunately their finances could fund neither. That summer Barbe had reached out to various contacts, hoping their influence could lead to scholarship money for Duncan. A number of people responded by writing letters on Duncan's behalf, including Harvard graduate and ACLU founder Supreme Court justice Felix Frankfurter. Barbe did not know Frankfurter personally, but a fellow union leader and family friend's strong endorsement of Duncan's record convinced him that Duncan was perfect Harvard material. When the two had embarked on their trip, hopes were high, but unfortunately sufficient funds failed to materialize. So instead of moving out, Duncan attended ISNU, worked at both a local drugstore and on campus, and lived at home. He led a more independent life, but it was not as free from oversight as he might have liked. Barbe continued to have expectations regarding his behavior. For example, nearly halfway through his second year, in a scene reminiscent of J. B.'s scolding twenty years earlier, Barbe took Duncan to task. He had stayed out until 1:25 a.m. at "some bowling place," and she felt compelled to give her nearly twenty-one-year-old son "a sound lecture" the next morning. Six months later, after Duncan took a local girl to the movies, Barbe informed him that she "didn't like it as we didn't have the money to spend on girls." So despite the assumption of change that Duncan's college life was to bring, in many ways Barbe's daily life between 1939 and 1941 stayed the same. She continued to balance work, home, and parenting with activism.[3]

One big difference did finally emerge, however, as her expanded activism finally culminated in some late-1930s and early-1940s victories. In 1939 the Illinois General Assembly finally repealed the inadequate 1915 pension legislation. In its stead, they passed new legislation that pegged contributions to salaries, ensuring more substantial and guaranteed retirement benefits. In 1941 another victory came when the combined efforts of the IEA, IFT, and numerous downstate teachers' groups finally succeeded in gaining statewide tenure legislation. This law provided continuous contract protection to teachers with two years' consecutive service in one school district. School boards now had to provide a specific legal reason ("just cause") in writing for dismissals or failures to renew contracts, and teachers had the right to appeal both. These victories were gratifying, but not all battles were won.

By 1939 the local Bloomington Federation had joined with state education organizations such as the IFT and the IEA as well as the WTUL to aggressively lobby for changes in school taxation limits. Barbe's bond with Agnes Nestor was helpful in this fight, as she lent her nationally recognized voice in support of the desired "Unit Bill." This bill would provide a way for Illinois school districts on the unit system (grades one through twelve under one governing board) to raise local assessment rates on real estate to a preset limit without referendum. Proponents argued that these funds would allow unit schools to come up to par with nonunit schools (which had less stringent tax limits) by extending school from nine to ten months, standardizing salaries, and expanding the curriculum. From 1939 to 1941, Barbe repeatedly journeyed to Springfield to lobby for the bill, but time after time it failed to get out of the general assembly. In May and June 1941, supporters staged a final big push. Barbe wrote letters, made telephone calls, and appeared at least once before a senate committee. In late June, victory was achieved when the assembly passed the bill. Unfortunately, their joy was short-lived, as the newly elected Republican governor, Dwight Green, vetoed it. This upsetting turn of events left Bloomington school funding in the hands of local voters, whose demands for better schools did not always coalesce with their demands for lower taxes.

In the midst of the battle at the state level, Barbe continued her work closer to home, much to the appreciation of local unionists. As Chicago teachers' union leader John Walker pointed out at a local Democratic Party rally for labor in October 1940, Barbe was a "fine citizen who helped organize teachers."[4] But praise did nothing to mitigate the reality of another recent Bloomington tax referendum defeat in the spring of 1940, followed closely by the Unit Bill veto. Nor did it help to lift her mood when the school board rejected a spring 1941 request for a return to 1931 salary rates. The US economy had begun a slow rise, as the United States implemented efforts to supply the Allied forces in the war already raging overseas. This initial recovery meant rising prices, while teachers' wages remained stuck at drastically reduced Depression rates. In the face of this immediate income disparity, the recently won future pension-protection benefits paled in importance, especially as employee pension-contribution payments came directly out of their already strained monthly paychecks. No solution seemed imminent. Then the December 1941 bombing of Pearl Harbor brought the United States directly into the world war.

The war raged for another four years, and as many as 75 million soldiers and civilians lost their lives. It also wreaked havoc on the infrastructures and economies of most of the involved nations. For the United States, however, the rapid rise of industrial war-material output brought the Depression to an abrupt end. The now booming war economy reduced the opposition to the idea of higher taxes for schools. The school board quickly responded to this shift and scheduled a referendum on raising real estate assessments for the purposes of education. As the chair of both the BFT and the Parent-Teacher Association legislative committees, Barbe devoted a lot of time and effort to campaigning for this referendum. Plus, as a member of her union's salary committee, she drafted the petition laying out teachers' expectations. They demanded immediate raises for all teachers as well as a uniform (less arbitrary) salary schedule. They also added an ultimatum of sorts: they wanted raises regardless of the referendum outcome, and if the money ran out, then schools should be closed until the teachers could be paid their full salaries.

The union had made a similar threat in 1934, but realistically (also like 1934) the teachers had little power to force this outcome. They really needed the referendum to pass. As she had in prior years, Barbe aggressively electioneered for the tax vote, but this time the union had the help of the WTUL. She and local WTUL president Mary White spent hours comparing real estate assessment lists with phone lists so they could target those voters who did not own property, hoping they would be more amenable to a yes vote. All their hard work paid off, as the referendum victory also echoed 1934. Despite this victory, however, the school board refused to provide immediate raises. Members were angered, but in reality the union had little actual recourse. They still had no legal bargaining power, and although the new tenure law did offer added security, no laws protected striking teachers or no-shows. In fact, state law prohibited both types of labor activism by public employees. So they did not push for forced closings, but they did push for talks. After a contentious month of discussions between the board and the salary committee, a "compromise" was reached. The teachers were promised a flat $175 raise on their following year's contracts. A fairer set salary schedule was also implemented, which based their wages on education and training instead of the grade level taught, ending, in part, the system in which college-educated grade school teachers like Barbe made significantly less than high school teachers regardless of tenure or education. Despite this positive change, however, women's salaries remained fixed below men's, regardless of grade level.

During the same period that Barbe had fought for the (ultimately vetoed) Unit Bill and the victorious tax referendum, Duncan transferred to the University of Illinois for his final year of college. His departure in September 1941 marked the last time he lived at home, and Barbe struggled to face his impending absence. The day he left, she stayed home to "prepare a decent meal" before she drove him to Champaign, helped him unpack, and put away his things in the "tiny room." After a very brief tour of the campus, she drove home alone and faced the empty house. He frequently came home for one-day weekend visits (and his laundry arrived every week without fail), but she sorely missed his daily presence, and without him the "house seems so vacant."[5] He once again excelled in his studies, and nine months later he graduated, prepared to take a proffered accounting position at the prestigious firm of Arthur Andersen in Chicago. The day after graduation, however, Duncan reported to the draft office in Peoria. He and Arthur Andersen hoped to avoid the unknowns of a possible future military draft. Plus, he was confident that the army would reject him because of his asthma. Barbe had also been confident, but to her horror the following day Duncan sent word that he had been accepted into the service and was already at Scott Field in Belleville, Illinois. His college degree and army test scores resulted in cryptography and language training that kept him out of combat, but the secretiveness required for this program meant only highly censored letters that left Barbe far too much in the dark. Without even his weekly laundry to distract her from his absence, she devoted even more time to her labor activism.

For many women, World War II brought significant changes and new experiences. Millions of women entered the workforce or the military for the first time, obtained jobs never before available, took on volunteer roles outside the home, or stepped in as the head of the family when husbands and fathers went to war. For Barbe, the changes were not so obvious. Her lack of knowledge about Duncan's day-to-day life (and paucity of letters) agitated Barbe, but working, activism, and running the household on her own were not new experiences. A trip to Brunswick, Georgia, to take part in the christening of the US Liberty ship the SS *John Brown Lennon* did provide a novel and gratifying experience, especially as both she and J. B. were lauded for their contributions to the labor cause. But for the most part, Barbe's wartime experiences were less about change than expansion of her preexisting roles. She once again was taking classes (a Spanish class through an adult education program and then home economic extension courses), and she continued her work as a teacher. As in World War I, teachers were expected to take on additional roles, and Barbe helped register military volunteers, organize cards for the rationing board, and oversee student efforts to collect metal scraps (aluminum, brass, bronze, and copper). But it was her activist organization work that filled much of her time.

As in the prewar years, the teachers' union remained one of Barbe's main avenues of activism. The BFT had experienced a slight drop in numbers and fervor since the late 1930s, but a core group of women kept the group on task. Barbe served on the union's Executive Board and salary committee for most of the war's duration, and pay remained a central issue. After the small 1942 bump in pay, the salary committee continued their pressure on the school board. With assists from the booming wartime economy and the funds now coming in from the raised assessments, they finally saw some better results. In 1943 a pay raise brought Barbe's salary to just over its pre-Depression level of fourteen hundred dollars per year. Unfortunately, with wartime inflation teachers still had less buying power than during the Depression; plus, these raises still failed to address the gender inequity. So the union did not give up. The following year, they again pushed for gender equity, but the board justified its continued opposition with the familiar trope that men needed to be paid higher salaries if schools wanted to keep and replace male teachers. Finally, in April 1945, the school board, under the direction of a newly hired school superintendent, adopted a truly uniform salary schedule. It mandated that teachers of equivalent education, experience, and teaching load receive equal pay regardless of sex. Plus, it also finally got rid of the longtime policy against hiring or retaining married women.

In 1892 a resolution for equal pay for equal work could not even get a "second" to enable a vote of the Bloomington School Board. Fifty-three years later, more equitable wages and career opportunities finally arrived for Bloomington's female teachers, putting them ahead of many downstate Illinois teachers who would have to fight for several more years for pay equity. The BFT's continued pressure played a major role in this victory, but changing times also factored. While school boards had been preoccupied with losing male teachers, women began to leave, or simply not choose, the teaching profession. A variety of factors played a part in this shift, including the low pay, more stringent certification requirements, and growing numbers of other job opportunities for women, especially during the war. To stave off a looming teacher shortage, school boards began to be more amenable to women's salary demands. These salary wins capped off a half decade of victories that included the improved pension system, tenure protection for all Illinois public school teachers, and a higher professional standing. To some, the major battles seemed to be over. But Barbe's active involvement in groups focused on national interests meant she knew bigger issues remained on the horizon.

The WTUL, in particular, promised battles on a stage bigger than a local school board. Her role within the WTUL had already expanded far beyond its Depression-era boundaries when Agnes Nestor reached out in 1942 and asked Barbe to take the presidency of the Bloomington branch. Soon after that step, the Illinois WTUL elected her as secretary-treasurer of the state branch. For the duration of the war and beyond, these roles competed with work, household, and union activities for her time. As local president, she presided over monthly meetings as well as myriad other tasks. As secretary-treasurer of the state chapter, she frequently took day trips to Chicago for meetings and spent hours each week balancing the books and drafting letters seeking support for the WTUL's goals. As a delegate for both the local and the state branches, she attended conferences where diverse topics were addressed. For example, a November 1944 conference covered issues that included free trade and the problems of war workers. She even found time while serving as an IEA delegate at the December 1944 NEA convention in Washington, DC, to visit the AFL national offices and meet with WTUL national leader Elizabeth Christman to discuss national labor issues. In short, as Barbe's political lobbying efforts expanded beyond the local school board or state representatives, her commitment to broad-based changes deepened. As the nation moved forward in the postwar world, this commitment guided much of her efforts, as she also looked to the future.

9

Political Battles Won and Lost, 1945–1950

On August 14, 1945, the Japanese accepted the Allied peace terms, and Bloomington like the rest of "the U.S. went wild. . . . Employees threw papers and desks out of windows. . . . Downtown streets were white with paper."[1] The United States emerged from this jubilation at war's end in better shape than any other involved nation. The mainland saw no fighting and defense industry spending had spurred economic growth, while Europe and Asia endured frontline battles and massive bombing campaigns that left their infrastructures and economies shattered. Plus, in sheer numbers, the three hundred thousand Americans lost in combat paled in comparison to the millions of soldiers and civilians lost by other countries. Despite this seemingly strong foundation, the American economy entered an immediate postwar slump that many feared meant the return of the Depression. These economic fears along with emerging concerns about the spread of Soviet communism contributed to a sense of uncertainty regarding the best future path for America. By the early 1950s, those latter fears contributed to a swing away from liberalism and toward political and social conservatism, while the booming economy led many to forget their immediate postwar economic worries. But before the United States entered these conservative boom years, the country struggled to find its postwar footing. Within that context, Barbe took part in a variety of fights that provide a glimpse of the issues that the 1950s economic (and baby) boom only temporarily put on the back burner.

The end of the war began on a high personal note for Barbe when six weeks after the Japanese surrender, Duncan mustered out of the army and came home. That joy quickly gave way to disappointment, however, when only two weeks after his return he moved to Chicago to begin his long-ago-offered job with Arthur Andersen. Despite the company's efforts to retain him, only two years later he gave up this position to enter Harvard's law school. While at Arthur Andersen, Duncan had traveled extensively, so his rare visits were joyful times for Barbe. Once law school took him to faraway Boston, she saw him even less frequently, although his laundry continued to arrive each week via mail without fail. The paucity of their visits meant that Barbe had little intimate knowledge of his daily life, so she was surprised by his April 1949 letter announcing his engagement and planned June 1951 wedding. She was initially underwhelmed by this news, as she noted, "Many things can happen in two years." But when this relationship began to infringe on their rare time together, she became less cavalier. Duncan's choice to spend a summer break at a "cottage with Pat's people at Nantucket" elicited a sharp reaction from Barbe: "I don't like it. They are not people of his kind."[2]

Much to her relief, the relationship ended the following spring, but that gratification was short-lived. One month after the broken engagement, Duncan informed his mother that after his May 1950 graduation, he was returning to Arthur Andersen and bringing along another young woman, Carroll, to whom he was newly engaged. Both pieces of news were disheartening. Barbe believed the engagement too hasty after his very recent breakup, and she had hoped he would take a proffered ISNU position upon his graduation. She shared her thoughts, but to no avail. Duncan could not be swayed. He took the Arthur Andersen job and moved to Chicago, and in October 1950 the couple married. For Duncan, change defined those five years between mustering out and marriage, but for Barbe continuity held sway. Long-distance fretting over Duncan's welfare mirrored her worries during his enlistment, while work and politicking continued to dominate her daily life.

Her political activism continued to grow from the roots planted in the prior five years. By the early 1940s, she had moved from electioneering and lobbying only at the local level to electioneering and lobbying at the state and federal levels. Her focus had also widened. She had pushed for statewide laws tied to her career (educational taxation and teachers pensions), but she also actively worked for the rights of others. Along with efforts to protect female laborers, she had lobbied for the passage of an Illinois Railroad Retirement Act and an Illinois sealed-records adoption law designed to reduce the stigma attached to unwed mothers and "illegitimate" children. At the federal level, she fought to extend inadequate and arbitrary Aid to Dependent Children and Social Security coverage and to increase funding for the Women's Bureau. In the five years following the war's end, she continued to believe in the possibilities of pragmatic liberalism, but political activism took an even more central role in her efforts. As part of that hopeful outlook, she devoted considerable energy working with local and state Illinois Democratic Women (IDW).

Barbe had helped organize a local branch of Democratic Illinois women in 1934, but her growing commitment to hands-on participation had come in 1944 when she worked to get fellow Unitarian and liberal Democrat Emily Taft Douglas elected to the United States House of Representatives. Barbe had first met Emily's husband, Paul H. Douglas, when he spoke for the Bloomington-Normal Forum in November 1941. His rousing speech condemned the Nazi campaign to pit Jew against Christian, white against black, and foreign born against native born, and he warned of a frightening Hitler-run world with no unions but plenty of concentration camps. Barbe thought him brilliant. After narrowly losing the 1942 US Senate race, he enlisted (at age fifty) in the military. During her husband's absence, Emily Douglas also stepped into the political ring and in 1944 ran against an isolationist candidate for an Illinois House seat.

During that campaign, Barbe took part in the large Democratic rallies meant to build support and enthusiasm, but she also participated in "teas" with smaller select groups of women for the purposes of both raising money for candidates and women's awareness re- garding Democratic-supported issues. Emily Douglas defeated her opponent in that election, but the dominating wins by Democratic candidates, which the Depression and war had wrought, had peaked. Once the war was over, the fight to determine the country's direction escalated. Liberal Democrats, like Douglas, found it more difficult to convince the majority to back their vision of the future. Barbe, however, remained convinced, and she devoted considerable time and energy battling to build momentum and support for important liberal issues. Not surprisingly, those liberal Democratic issues often dove- tailed with the goals of the WTUL. Both lobbied for the proposed United Nations and supported the United Nations Relief and Reha- bilitation Administration's work with displaced peoples. (The latter organization predated the UN but became part of it after it was char- tered.) But the needs of those closer to home also garnered attention from both groups during this same time period.

   In the immediate postwar years, local Democratic women and the WTUL worked to support pending anti–poll tax legislation that would eliminate a required fee ("poll tax") in order to vote. By the 1930s, the poll tax had emerged as an important civil rights issue because of its widespread use in the South to block the black vote. But it was also considered a women's issue, as it was understood that if a poor house- hold could afford only one voting tax, then the husband usually took that spot, effectively disenfranchising lower-class woman. The poll-tax debate also revealed the divide between liberal and conservative mem- bers within both parties. In 1942 and 1944, the US House of Represen- tatives passed anti–poll tax bills with bipartisan support, only to have them killed by filibustering southern Democrats. In the summer of 1945, the bill once again was under consideration. Illinois did not have poll taxes, but local Democratic women as well as the WTUL firmly supported a federal ban, as did the liberal wings of both the Demo- cratic and the Republican Parties. Once again Barbe went to work lob- bying her Illinois congressmen as well as the president. At the request of national WTUL leader Elizabeth Christman, she even reached out to Republican whip and Illinois native Leslie Arends in an attempt to circumvent the filibuster. He refused to help. Instead, he chose loyalty to the obstructionist southern Democrats that were the other half of a powerful voting coalition made up of conservative Republicans in the North and conservative Democrats in the South. This attempt's outcome mirrored the two prior efforts (as would a 1948 attempt): the bill passed in the House but was quashed by a conservative filibuster in the Senate. This liberal-conservative divergence would have long-term effects. It would temporarily splinter the Democratic Party in 1948 and eventually lead southern Democrats to permanently abandon the party during the civil rights debates of the 1960s.

In those five years after the war, another divisive fight also demanded WTUL attention. From its earliest days, the WTUL had staunchly maintained support for protective labor legislation for women. Support for those laws had swayed as societal views regarding women's appropriate roles changed, but, ironically, some of the WTUL's fiercest opposition had come from other women's rights supporters. Fundamental differences in the definitions of equality explained this rift. Women's labor activists, like Barbe, did not believe women to be inferior; nonetheless, she did believe that protective legislation that placed limits on an employer's ability to exploit women workers and their biological differences was the best way to achieve actual equality in the labor force. Unfortunately, this argument's reliance on the notion of fundamental differences between men and women directly countered the belief in absolute human equality championed by another strand of women's rights proponents. The differences between these two ways of viewing the fight for equality came to the forefront in the wake of the 1920 suffrage victory when the National Woman's Party introduced the Equal Rights Amendment (ERA). This proposed amendment simply stated that equality could not be denied because of sex. Fearing this kind of unmitigated legal equality threatened to undo any and all protective legislation, women labor activists had aggressively fought its passage. In their view, higher wages and a better working environment for women superseded any ideological focus on gender equality.

Throughout the 1920s and 1930s, labor activists had the ear of most women's rights supporters, and the ERA languished. But in the 1940s, many of the women's organizations that had previously stood in opposition began to shift their positions. Women's professional and business organizations were the first, but in 1944 the General Federation of Women's Clubs joined the ERA lobby. The massive federation had been a longtime protective legislation proponent, so its switch was a blow to ERA opponents. In subsequent years, favorable committee votes in Congress set the stage for a full congressional vote in 1946. Despite the ERA's growing number of backers, however, the League of Woman Voters, the WTUL, and labor-supporting Democrats remained staunchly opposed. Barbe set out in September 1945 to make sure that message was heard, starting at the top, by sending a strongly worded letter to President Truman protesting the ERA. She followed that with petitions, letters, and calls to her senators. In June and July 1946, as the July 19 vote approached, these missives escalated. In the end, this hard work paid off, as the amendment received a majority vote in the Senate but not the two-thirds required. The Illinois WTUL *Bulletin* proudly noted that neither the Republican nor the Democratic senator from Illinois voted yes on the "so-called 'Equal Rights' Amendment . . . due to the good work done through our organizations throughout the state."[3]

The victory was satisfying, but another battle was already under way. During that same summer and fall of 1946, Emily Taft Douglas was also campaigning for reelection. Barbe worked with the Democratic women's group, as she had in the previous campaign, but she also used her WTUL affiliation to bring Douglas's message to a wider audience. In October the Illinois and Wisconsin branches of the WTUL held a conference in Chicago. Barbe helped organize this summit, and Douglas served as a keynote speaker. Attendees celebrated the recent ERA defeat, but they also focused on pending labor legislation, price-control issues, and reforming the Social Security Act—all issues in which Douglas and the WTUL were in accord. Unfortunately, WTUL support was not enough to sway the majority. Douglas lost her bid for reelection, as did many Democrats. Control of Congress shifted to the Republicans for the first time since Hoover's presidency. This swing led to other disappointments for the WTUL and liberal Democrats who supported New Deal–style social legislation, unions, and civil rights. Unions took the first hit.

Postwar economic instability in which rapidly rising prices were not matched by rising wages had contributed to a surge of strikes. Historically, Republicans had been less than supportive of labor, but now they aggressively condemned the recent labor unrest, and the new Congress introduced hundreds of labor bills designed to lessen union power. The Taft-Hartley Act held the most potential danger to union strength with its limits on strikes, boycotts, picketing, and closed shops. Labor went to work to stop it. The WTUL did its part in lobbying against the bill while also making sure to get its message out regarding the bill's tangential threats. As the Illinois WTUL noted, the fight forced attention away from other pressing matters. Instead of working to improve conditions for Americans by lobbying to expand Social Security or raise the minimum wage, energy had to be diverted to the opposition of the antilabor bills.

In May 1947, Barbe traveled to a national WTUL convention in Washington, DC, to do just that. Her participation in this conference was almost derailed, however, when in April she lost her position as treasurer of the Illinois WTUL. Barbe missed the one-day conference in Springfield where the vote took place (because she failed to obtain permission to miss a school day). She angrily accused Illinois WTUL president Mary White of failing to inform her of the pending vote and ultimately blamed her for the loss. Her accusations may have had foundation. Their earlier congenial acquaintance had devolved into a somewhat contentious personal and professional relationship. Barbe felt White (as president) devoted insufficient time and effort to the state branch while simultaneously downplaying the influence of the Bloomington branch. She shared this opinion with national WTUL figures (and friends) Agnes Nestor and Elizabeth Christman on more than one occasion, a fact of which White was no doubt aware. Despite Barbe's demotion from the state board, Christman sent a personal message urging Barbe to attend, and the local branch (wanting to be part of this effort) managed to raise the money for the trip.

Upon her arrival in DC, she spent several hours getting reacquainted with the city (after a recent visit for the 1944 NEA conference) before a predinner meeting with national WTUL president Rose Schneiderman and vice president Mary Dreier. The following day, she enjoyed a cruise on the Potomac and talked with Elizabeth Christman before having lunch with both Schneiderman and Dreier. First thing the next morning, Barbe, along with several other WTUL women, had the honor of meeting with First Lady Bess Truman in the Blue Room of the White House. After this visit, the conference officially got under way. Featured speakers included the AFL legislative director, the executive director of the Women's Division of the Democratic National Committee, the secretary-treasurer of the CIO, and the director of the Women's Bureau. Barbe attended many of the forums, including "The Woman Worker: What Laws Does She Need and How Can We Get Them?" and "The Woman Worker: What Education Programs Will Benefit Her?" As a member of the Education Committee, she also worked on rewriting a resolution for the latter regarding recommended local WTUL labor school classes. She and other Illinois delegates also made a visit to Capitol Hill to meet with the Democratic senator regarding pending legislation, including the Taft-Hartley Act. Barbe came away from this conference energized. Unfortunately, labor's continued hard work failed to sway the Republican-led Congress, and the Taft-Hartley Act passed over President Truman's veto in late June 1947.

During this same period when labor unions battled nationally for their continued existence, Bloomington teachers also struggled. Economically, Barbe's 1945 raise still left her 50 percent below the average income for a head of household, while at the same time her workload had grown. Recent changes in the Bloomington school by-laws had expanded classroom teachers' responsibilities, which meant more committees, more meetings, and more paperwork. For Barbe, the Curriculum Committee, in particular, demanded significant time and effort. She often complained about the workload, especially the required documentation, and noted frequently that she was "so tired and discouraged. Too much required of us at school."[4] This complaint echoed nationwide, as surveys found teachers felt buried under the sheer amount of required clerical work, which left little time for grading or working with individual students. In Bloomington, as in most districts, this extra work was not met with extra pay or authority. The teachers' union still had no legal bargaining rights, which hampered efforts to push for fair compensation. But the BFT's diminishing numbers likely also weakened their position. Antiunion sentiment contributed to a drop in membership from a peak of 170 during the worst of the Depression to only about 60 in 1947.

Despite the BFT's weakening strength and numbers, the BTLA remained committed to the teachers' union. The labor association took up the teachers' wage cause and publicly chastised the superintendent of schools for his unwillingness to bargain with the teachers on salaries. Whether this public dressing-down affected the board, however, is unclear. Two months later, in May 1947, the board renewed contracts, and did boost salaries, but it also extended the school year from nine to ten months. Barbe's pay rose to $2,250, but the longer term meant her monthly raise totaled only $70. As low as her wages remained, at least Bloomington's female teachers had pay equity, which many other women workers still lacked. That inequity kept women's rights and labor activists fighting for a change both at the state and at the national levels. Toward that goal, in April 1947, backers introduced an Equal Pay Bill in the Illinois General Assembly. It got some favorable feedback and a positive vote out of committee before being stricken from the calendar in July before it could even be voted on. Equal-pay legislation was also introduced into the US Congress in July 1947. It also got no traction. In an effort to draft strategies to reignite the fight, labor activists gathered at the WTUL Interstate Conference in Chicago in November 1947. Two champions of the cause spoke: a former Democratic congresswomen and a current Illinois Republican state representative. Both women had introduced equal-pay legislation, only to be stymied by bipartisan conservative opposition, despite the fact that both parties publicly advocated equal pay for women. Barbe was inspired by both women, but ultimately conservative opposition proved stronger than party rhetoric. Universal pay equity, as well as a considerable number of other hopeful pieces of liberal legislation, remained unfulfilled goals over the next two decades.

But the ultimate demise of the 1940s liberal agenda was not yet clear in 1948. In fact, in early 1948, Barbe saw hope in the release of the presidential commission on civil rights report *To Secure These*

Rights. This report included recommendations for anti–poll tax legislation, antilynching legislation, a permanent Fair Employment Practices
Commission, and desegregation of the military. But the hope of that
report remained largely unfulfilled. Truman desegregated the military
with an executive order, but unfortunately, like equal pay, the others
remained stuck in the Republican-led Congress with obstructionist
help from southern Democrats. The question became whether these
setbacks signaled wavering national support for New Deal–style liberal
ideas or simply reflected superior political strategizing by the minority.
This uncertainty lent the 1948 election import, as moderately conservative Republican Thomas Dewey took on the Democratic incumbent,
Harry S. Truman, in the presidential race. With Truman's approval rat-
ings low, victory for the Democrats seemed a long shot.

At the state level, however, the candidacies of Illinois Democrats
Paul H. Douglas and Adlai Stevenson II offered liberals hope. Democratic women in particular stepped up to show their support, as they
answered the call to action made by a Democratic state chairwom-
an's recurring "Women in Politics" speech. Barbe's experience illustrates one facet of that hopeful participation. She actively supported
both Douglas's bid for US senator and Stevenson's run for Illinois
governor. But the latter had special significance for Barbe, as he was
Bloomington raised and a fellow Unitarian. She was not alone in her
admiration, and in January 1948 Barbe, along with the local Democratic Women's Division, met to plan their work for the Stevenson
campaign at the mansion home of Julia Vrooman. Vrooman and her
husband (a former secretary of agriculture under Woodrow Wilson)
were longtime liberal Democratic supporters, and Stevenson was Julia
Vrooman's cousin. Soon after this strategy session, Barbe and three
hundred other invitees attended Stevenson's official kickoff dinner,
and the campaign season was under way.

In February 1948, Barbe's time commitment intensified when she
was elected secretary of the McLean County chapter of the Illinois
Democratic Women (IDW) and then two months later was chosen
as a McLean County delegate to the Democratic state convention. As
part of these varied Democratic roles, she attended planning meetings
and cheered at rallies, but as a board member of the IDW she also

took part in several dinners where the smaller numbers allowed a less cursory candidate meet-and-greet. Plus, throughout the campaign, the Illinois Democratic Women organized separate events to allow women expanded opportunities. For example, Barbe took part in a large conference in which approximately a thousand women met in Springfield to show support for Democratic candidates. Then only two days after that large rally, she and about fifty women met in Bloomington to work specifically on advancing Stevenson's campaign.

The state race remained hopeful, but nationally things did not look good for Democrats. Having chosen Dewey over more conservative choices, the Republicans mapped out what appeared to be a middle-ground majority, whereas the Democratic platform clearly represented its more liberal members. Both parties supported equal wages and expanded Social Security benefits while also being firmly anti-Communist at home and overseas, but from there they widely diverged. Unlike the Republicans, the Democrats were decisively prounion and advocated raising the minimum wage, establishing a national health program, using federal money for low-income housing, and providing federal aid to education. The platform also included a clear and aggressive civil rights plank. But as evidenced by southern Democrats' obstructionism on some of these same issues, not all Democrats ascribed to this form of liberalism. In July 1948, the Democratic National Convention devolved into a contentious brawl over the inclusion of the civil rights plank. An impromptu convention-floor parade led by Paul Douglas rallied enough support to have the plank accepted, but southern Democrats from Mississippi and Alabama proved unwilling to acquiesce. As a result, they walked out and nominated their own candidate (Strom Thurmond) under the newly founded Dixiecrat ticket. Plus, a faction of progressive liberals who advocated for a less belligerent stance toward the Soviet Union had already broken away to pledge their support for Henry Wallace.

While nationally Democrats battled a perception that losing the presidential race was inevitable, Barbe continued her work as a core member of the Stevenson campaign team. In October she was one of only twelve people strategizing at the local Stevenson headquarters on final plans for election day. In the week between that meeting and the election, she traveled to Milwaukee for a WTUL Interstate Conference, where discussions about labor's stake in civil rights also took center stage. She returned to Bloomington in time to vote and savor the election-day victory. Stevenson, Douglas, and—to the surprise of many—Truman had all proved winners. The latter's narrow victory was due in no small part to the Democratic turnout in Illinois. In January her active political support garnered invitations to Stevenson's inauguration and reception the following day, where she proudly noted she was the first to shake hands with fellow attendee and incoming US vice president Alben Barkley.

Throughout 1949 and into the 1950s, hoping to build on that winning momentum, she continued the fight alongside her fellow Illinois Democrats and WTUL members. And in the fall of 1949, they scored a victory when their efforts to pass a "Status of Women" bill yielded results. This bill, first introduced in 1947, was a version of an equal rights act that the WTUL (and labor activists like the Women's Bureau) could support. It called for "no distinctions on the basis of sex except such as are reasonably justified in physical structure, biological or social function."[5] It was meant as a direct substitute for the proposed ERA because it allowed for protective legislation. In January 1950, the original ERA again was under debate when (on the suggestion of the Women's Bureau) an Arizona senator offered a surprise rider to the original amendment, which simply added the provision that the ERA would not invalidate any current or future protective legislation. This rider clearly destroyed the intent and the power of the ERA, but it offered an "out" for legislators who wavered on the potential political fallout of voting (or not voting) for the original ERA. Much to the disappointment of ERA supporters (who were caught a bit off guard by this rider) and much to the satisfaction of WTUL members, this version passed. Barbe was thrilled. She even wrote a congratulatory note to Senator Douglas for his vote, for which she received a personal follow-up thank-you phone call.

In some ways, this vote and the call from Douglas represented an end of an era for Barbe. In the months following, signs of change were everywhere. In November 1949, she had taken a fall down a staircase at school (leaving her with multiple stitches and some muscle damage), and she had to miss her first WTUL Interstate Conference in years. In December 1949, Duncan celebrated the holidays with his then fiancée, setting a precedent for missed holidays in the future. Still suffering from the aftereffects of her November fall, in February 1950 she submitted her intent to retire at the end of the semester. The BFT also continued to shrink. A sense of diminishing returns along with a trend in which less radicalized teachers replaced rapidly retiring members left Barbe as one of only fifty BFT members in 1950. In April 1950, the Bloomington-Normal Forum Board began to talk about disbanding due to low ticket sales, as new forms of entertainment, especially television, were becoming more popular. Then in May 1950, she learned only a month after his broken engagement to Pat that Duncan had set a date to marry Carroll and had taken the Arthur Andersen position in Chicago. That news was followed a week later by Elizabeth Christman's letter telling Barbe that due to a lack of funds, the national WTUL was going out of existence. In early June 1950, she submitted her request for pension paperwork, cleaned out her classroom, and attended a retirement reception at Allerton Park, where she and three other teachers were honored. Her days as a Bloomington School District teacher were now officially over.

In June 1902, she had graduated from Bloomington High School and began teaching with rather narrow expectations, but in the nearly half a century since that day, she had widened her path in myriad ways. Now, as she walked out those school doors, her course seemed to be narrowing once again, as change began to close many of the doors that had led to wider opportunity. Her next challenge would be to navigate and work to widen this narrowing path. The summer offered a sense of brief respite from this challenge, as it mirrored, in many ways, prior school breaks. She worked on housecleaning neglected during the winters, tended her garden, lobbied at the behest of the Women's Bureau director, attended union events, and continued her work with the Democratic women's organization. But this familiar routine could not stop the inevitable changes looming at summer's end when Duncan would marry and the school year would start without her. The former occupied her mind, as she continued to feel it was a bad decision. She thought the timing hasty, but she was also unimpressed with his fiancée. She tried to persuade him to postpone, but after realizing that he was "bound to go through with it," she finally accepted its inevitability.[6] She even gave him the ring J. B. had given her thirty years prior to give to Carroll. As summer closed, Barbe made the trip to the Florida home of the bride's parents for the wedding and then returned to Bloomington to tackle a new phase of her life. For the first time in nearly fifty years, her time was not structured around the primary roles of teacher or mother. She struggled a bit at first, but before long she embraced new versions of her old roles as mother, teacher, and activist in ways that illustrate both continuity and change.

10

Continuity and Change, 1950–1983

Barbe filled the years after her retirement with a wide variety of activities that reflected and built on the interests developed over the prior sixty-plus years of her life. And for nearly thirty of those years, mothering Duncan had been central. In some ways, her role after Duncan married remained remarkably similar to her role before: she worried. She fretted over his health and his work schedule and increasingly over his happiness. Unfortunately, this latter worry manifested in ways that often put a wedge between the two. Discussions with Carroll's elderly aunt at the couple's wedding had affirmed Barbe's fear that Carroll was a lazy spendthrift. Barbe wrote Duncan numerous "personal" letters (often in German so Carroll could not read them) in which she demanded information to calm her fears, but he remained taciturn. Plus, on the infrequent occasions she saw the couple, Carroll's attitude seemed to indicate that she shared an equally low opinion of her mother-in-law. For three years, visits were rare. Whether this was simply a function of Duncan's travel schedule, the women's shared disdain, or marital discord is unknown, but in hindsight Barbe may have been right to worry. In June 1953, Duncan wrote his mother to share the news that his "very unhappy marriage" was ending in divorce. In keeping with her consistent attitude about Carroll,

Barbe's reaction was succinct. She was "glad he was rid of . . . [that] adventuress."[1] For the next two years, she enjoyed Duncan's more frequent postdivorce visits, but in May 1955 he married again, and their dynamic once again shifted. Initially, she and his new wife, Barbara (Barbi), enjoyed a congenial relationship, but it did not last. In October 1955, the newlywed couple's somewhat ambivalent reaction to the news of Barbi's pregnancy upset Barbe. The ensuing argument inserted tensions that never really resolved. Three grandsons arrived in rather quick succession, and although they remained in communication over the next decade, years passed without a visit.

As her active role as mother shifted somewhat from the center, she also grappled with establishing a satisfying daily life. Her retirement meant she no longer served in leadership positions for professional support organizations such as the IEA or the BFT. And even her honorary place within her local teacher federation diminished as the union continued to dissolve. By 1959 the BFT's last year on record, only ten members remained, and when local teachers finally did organize as a recognized bargaining unit more than a decade later it would be under the auspices of the NEA, not the AFT. But this lacuna did not go unfilled. As the years unfolded, she energetically pushed open new doors as others closed. She served on the Executive Board of the McLean County Retired Teachers Association until well into the 1970s and continued to lobby for pension protection throughout. She also recommitted time to familiar interests. She returned to school as a student in a series of adult education classes while also serving on the program planning board. In the spring of 1951, she resumed her role as the secretary-treasurer of the Unitarian Alliance and the treasurer of the Unitarian Board. Socially, the A Volonte Club still met, but she also reenergized involvement with the DeMolay Mothers and joined a book club, the Bloomington-Normal History Club, the Garden Club, and the Home Bureau. She would remain involved to some degree with these groups for nearly all of the next thirty years. She also began volunteering at least once a week at the local hospital thrift shop (a job she would maintain until 1966). But two longtime interests—politics and teaching—dominated much of her time in both old and new ways.

The local WTUL branch had chosen to stay together for several more years after the national folded, but the loss of those connections weakened its abilities to effect any real political change. It hobbled along for a couple of years, mainly as a fund-raising entity, so politically she now devoted much of her time to the Illinois Democrats and League of Women Voters. Locally, she lobbied for school board candidates and in support of adopting a city-manager form of government. In 1950 and 1951, she served again as a McLean County Democratic convention delegate and in 1952 and 1956 worked tirelessly for (the ultimately unsuccessful) Democratic presidential candidate, Adlai Stevenson. She devoted hours each day in the months before each election volunteering at the local Stevenson headquarters, campaigning door-to-door, and polling potential voters. Her efforts continued to be recognized by state Democrats and the Stevenson-Ives family, but the Democratic success of 1948 proved short-lived. By the early 1950s, Republicans had taken control at the local, state, and national levels. Nonetheless, she stayed committed to the liberal Democratic agenda, meaning she would not cast a vote for a winning candidate again until the 1960s, when her straight-Democratic ticket helped to elect John F. Kennedy and then Lyndon B. Johnson.

She also found ways to incorporate teaching into her life, despite the fact that her days as a district schoolteacher were behind her. Throughout the 1950s and into the 1960s, she periodically tutored students—both children and adults—from her home, but her involvement in another teaching effort took center stage during this same period. From 1952 until 1963, she worked as a volunteer for the local "Americanization" program, teaching English reading and language skills to immigrants. Her first students were a displaced Romanian family, and over the years she would add new arrivals from Austria, China, Puerto Rico, and Germany. She dedicated significant time and energy to this program, often teaching several nights a week. But it was not all work. Barbe attended students' birthday parties and weddings and witnessed numerous citizenship ceremonies. Participants, both students and teachers, often also gathered for field trips, holiday parties, and celebrations. This program connected her to a wide range of people and made a lasting impact on both student and teacher. She stayed in contact with many of her pupils over the years, as they established roots as newly minted Americans citizens.

Unlike her work with local immigrant populations, another project required her to travel to the students. Post-Reconstruction legal segregation in the South had produced an educational system in which minority students were relegated to vastly inferior separate schools. At the same time, poverty-stricken rural students (both whites and minorities) suffered from a lack of access to educational facilities. In response to these needs, a variety of religious and philanthropic organizations had stepped in to help—not by battling systematic segregation or the sources of poverty—but by offering schooling alternatives. Many of these mission schools survived into the twentieth century to serve the children and grandchildren of their original students. They provided educational opportunities still not widely available, particularly to nonwhite students. Between April 1952 and September 1955, Barbe and two other retired teachers embarked on eight extended trips into the South to observe, report, and advise a wide variety of these mission schools. On their first two-week trip, the women spent time at Warren Wilson College and Allen High School in North Carolina. Wilson had been founded to serve poor rural whites but had just recently voted to accept its first African American student (a full two years before *Brown v. Board of Education*), and Allen High was a boarding school for African American girls. Over the next few years, they added multiple visits to schools catering to minority students, including Philander Smith College in Arkansas, the Dulac Indian Mission and Dillard University in Louisiana, and the Piney Woods School, Rust College, and Gulfside School in Mississippi. Throughout these multiple tours, Barbe was struck by the poverty, the likes of which she had never seen, but she was even more impressed by the devotion and effort each institution had for its mission and its students. Even after the visits stopped, Barbe remained in contact with a variety of school administrators as well as several students. In particular, she and a young woman from the Dulac Indian Mission stayed in touch, corresponding for many years.

As these long trips illustrate, traveling played a significant role in Barbe's life, and (like thirty years prior) her car made much of that

autonomy possible. One of her first postretirement acts was to replace the Chevrolet she had been driving since the 1930s with a new
five-door Studebaker. Its seventeen-hundred-dollar cost was barely
mitigated by the fifty-dollar trade-in, but the extravagance proved
its worth over the years. In addition to the southern mission-school
tours, she drove to southern Florida several times to attend ISNU re-
unions hosted by transplants. She also made numerous shorter trips
to visit family in Odell and friends in Iowa. Plus, she often served as
chauffeur for in-town friends. This facet of her independence, however, slowly eroded over time. In 1954 she was forced to take both
the written and the driving parts of the licensing exam because of
her age. She proudly scored perfectly on the written portion, but it
took two tries to master the driving portion. And as the years passed,
minor accidents became more prevalent, including denting a fender
while backing out of her barn garage. By the late 1950s, she began to
limit her driving to mostly daytime and closer to home. But even after
she quit making long-distance drives, she continued to travel with
friends, taking extended trips to places such as Alaska, Canada, New
York City, and Florida via bus, train, boat, and plane. These adven-
tures added to the fullness of the fifteen or so years after Barbe's retirement. She maintained autonomy and a sense of individual identity, as
she had carved out new versions of her roles as mother, teacher, and
activist. Nevertheless, as the 1960s unfolded, incremental shifts began
to take effect.

Her age—she was now in her eighties—started to force a change
in her routines. Maintaining set weekly schedules with multiple daily
commitments proved tiring, so she let go of some things. She occasionally still tutored a student in her home, but her role as an Americanization teacher ended in 1964, and she gave up the thrift-shop
work in 1966. Although she remained a staunch Democratic supporter, by the early 1960s she had ceased playing an active role in
campaigning or electioneering. But curtailing these activities did not
mean she sat at home every day. She continued her involvement in
the History Club, Garden Club, DeMolay Mothers, Farm Bureau,
and the Retired Teachers Association as well as the A Volonte Club.
Her sight continued to trouble her, and she also had to start wearing

hearing aids, so she drove even more sparingly but also still took care of the housework, shoveled snow off her front path, mowed the lawn, weeded and planted her garden, and walked everywhere. Despite the necessity to limit some activities, throughout the 1960s and well into the 1970s, she lived an independent and busy life.

In the years after Duncan and Barbi's marriage, the dynamic of her role as mother shifted, as her relationship with Duncan and his family changed over time. Throughout the 1950s, Duncan had continued his extensive travel for work, and by the early 1960s he had relocated his family to Florida. Barbe and Barbi remained at odds, and for a decade visits remained rare. Then in early December 1964, tragedy brought an end to this dynamic, when Barbi died from carbon monoxide poisoning in an apparent suicide. Upon hearing the news, Barbe flew immediately to Florida and stayed for two weeks to help. She enjoyed the extended time with her grandsons, but at her age they were a lot to handle, and she was somewhat relieved to relinquish responsibility once Duncan hired full-time help. The entire family was hard hit by Barbi's death, but the tragedy seemed to have dissolved the tensions between mother and son. Barbe visited the boys several times over the next few years and even more frequently after they moved to North Carolina. She also seemed happy when Duncan remarried in 1966. Apparently, Barbe had finally achieved some sense of peace with Duncan's choices, and with that acceptance her role as mother, mother-in-law, and grandmother settled into one less fraught with friction.

As the 1960s drew to a close, Barbe's roles slowly narrowed again. She still endeavored to lead a full life, but age hampered her ability to engage as energetically as in the past. She continued as a long-distance grandmother and mother, while she also acted on her daily desire to maintain an identity as a teacher and activist. These latter activities, however, had become more select. She stayed involved with the History Club and the Retired Teachers Association as well as the Garden Club but slowly let go of most of her other commitments. Throughout most of the 1970s, she also maintained her autonomous status as a home owner, but advancing age brought inevitable change. As she moved well into her nineties, the house finally became too much for her to handle, and in 1977 she left the home she had lived in since 1900. She spent many of her last days in North Carolina before passing away in Bloomington in 1983, where she was laid to rest alongside J. B. and Juna. According to official records, she was just shy of ninety-nine years old, but in reality she likely had passed the century mark. And what a century it had been.

Barbara Egger Lennon was not famous, but she serves as one example of the many unknown women—past and present—whose lives deserve recognition. She lived a long and productive life, and her last will and testament and her obituary combine to provide an apt summary of the important facets of her historical legacy. She bequeathed a lump sum of money to the Unitarian Church. Its commitment to liberal social justice and equality had helped build a foundation for much of the ideological framework evident in her 1930s and 1940s activism and beyond. The remainder of her estate went to Duncan, with the direction that its proceeds fund her grandsons' college educations. She never did earn sufficient credits to turn her ISNU three-year diploma into a four-year bachelor's degree, but her time at ISNU changed her life, and she remained a lifelong believer in the importance of education. And finally, her short obituary notes the multiple roles that defined her life: wife, mother, teacher, and principal as well as a member of the Unitarian Church, the WTUL, and the AFT. Throughout her long life, she endeavored to balance those varied roles in a way that challenges traditional ideas about the supposedly simpler lives of pre-1970s white womanhood. Her story adds depth and complexity to our shared history and reminds us why we need to continue our quest to incorporate the lives of women into the story of the past.

Primary Sources

EXCERPT OF BARBE'S CONTRACT FOR HER SECOND YEAR OF TEACHING AT THE
ELDORADO SCHOOL IN MCLEAN COUNTY, ILLINOIS, SEPTEMBER 7, 1903

Barbara Egger Lennon Collection at the McLean County History Museum

TEACHER'S CONTRACT

It is hereby decreed, by and between the School directors of District No 80 County of Mc-
Lean State of Illinois, and Miss Barbara Egger a legally qualified teacher, that said teacher
is to teach, govern and conduct the common school of said district, to the best of her ability. . . . For a term of nine months, commencing on the 7th day of September AD, 1903 for
the sum of 40 dollars per school month. . . .

Provided, that in the case said Miss Barbara Egger should be dismissed from said
school . . . for incompetency, cruelty, negligence, immorality, or a violation of any of the
stipulations of this contract . . . she shall not be entitled to compensation. . . .

LETTER FROM R. J. RAILSBACK (REPRESENTING THE HOPEDALE SCHOOL BOARD) TO
J. B. LENNON REGARDING SEVERAL REQUESTS MADE BY J. B. ON BARBE'S BEHALF,
OCTOBER 31, 1904

Barbara Egger Lennon Collection at the McLean County History Museum

Dear Sir:

We have carefully considered the matter of giving Miss Egger leave of absence for four weeks
after consultation with our principal and find that it will be impossible to grant her request
much as we should like to do so. Miss Egger is giving excellent satisfaction in her work in
both discipline and instruction, has her room under perfect control and our experience with
former teachers in the same grades makes us feel that when we have a teacher that can have
discipline and yet retain the love and respect of her pupils we should keep her right where
they are. Of course we appreciate your feeling in the matter and the great opportunity such
a trip would be for Miss Egger but the principle of the greater good to the greatest number
and our duties and obligation as directors compel us to decide as we have.

The second matter to which you refer is something that it seems to me the young ladies could arrange themselves. I should be pleased to do anything I could to better the conditions of their boarding place but I fear their landlady would consider it unwarranted interference on my part. I think that if they could speak to her about it that some way could be arranged for them to have a warm room to study in. Hoping that Miss Egger may have an opportunity later to make the California trip and assuring you that it is with a feeling of great reluctance that we refuse to grant her this favor, I am

Very Respectfully,

R. J. Railsback

EXCERPT FROM "TEACHERS AND THEIR DUTIES," IN *RULES OF THE BOARD OF EDUCATION, BLOOMINGTON, ILLINOIS, 1905–1911*

Section 1. Teachers elected by the Board may be required to teach in any part of the city or in any department that, in the judgment of the Board, the interests of the school demand, and may be changed from one school to another whenever the Board shall think such change for the interest of the schools.

Sec. 2. Whenever the records of the Supervisors and principal shall show that any teacher is incompetent . . . with the approval of the ward committee-man . . . be discharged. . . .

Sec. 3. Any teacher may resign his position, provided three weeks' notice of such intention be given. . . . In case a teacher shall leave without giving such notice, all unpaid salary shall be withheld. . . .

Sec. 5. Teachers who are sick shall receive half pay. . . . In case a teacher is absent on account of sickness in the family, no pay shall be allowed. . . .

Sec. 6. Teachers shall be in their respective rooms at least twenty minutes before the time for commencing the morning. . . .

Sec. 7. No teacher shall be absent from any teachers' meeting. . . . Teachers not answering to roll call at the first general teachers' meeting on Saturday preceding the opening of school shall forfeit pay. . . .

Sec. 9. No teacher shall engage in other work. . . .

Sec. 12. No teacher shall vary the prescribed course of study or use in school other than the adopted text-books. . . .

Sec. 13. It shall be the duty of the teacher to furnish a monthly report of attendance, deportment, and scholarship of each pupil to the parent. . . .

DOCUMENT SET 2: FAMILY

JOURNAL EXCERPTS. (ALL ORIGINAL SPELLING AND USAGE IS RETAINED.
BRACKETED COMMENTS ARE INSERTED ONLY IF NECESSARY FOR CLARITY.)

Barbara Egger Lennon Collection at the McLean County History Museum

August 3, 1907

. . . Mamsie [Juna Lennon] wrote letter. . . . Does not say a word about me coming home. Their letters sound as if they'd like to get rid of me—only they don't say it out plainly.

October 28, 1907

. . . One of the unhappiest days of my life. . . . Paying daddie [J. B. Lennon] thirty dollars on the loan of last summer. . . . Mamsie [Juna Lennon] heard and immediately began a tirade of abuse—said I'd better find a different home and called me sly and unreliable. Couldn't eat my dinner. Just before leaving for school said I expected too much of them and that they didn't always want me along. I didn't know I ever went along very much with them. . . . Mamsie very cool, hasn't spoken a word to me all evening—acts as if I were a dog.

February 4, 1908

. . . don't believe Mrs. L [Juna Lennon] wants me along with them. She said so much last November about my thinking I had to go wherever they did, that I'm afraid to suggest this.

August 8, 1908

. . . Don't enjoy going visiting for several weeks when I have work that must be done. Besides would like to visit in Odell and Hopedale and not H[annibal] but she [Juna] seems set on my going down there—if one doesn't do as she says—there is trouble.

August 10, 1908

. . . Would love to go [to Hopedale to visit] but know Mrs. L would be furious if I went there and not to her sisters [in Hannibal]. . . .

August 15, 1908

. . . Mother [Barbe's birth mother] and Frieda [Barbe's sister] aren't well and want to see me—am not free to go right away as Mrs. L would be furious—but I am worried about ma and would like to go right away. . . .

December 8, 1908

This morning upon arising Mrs. L asked if I had put the blanket on my bed. . . . I had hurriedly looked for it, but couldn't find it. She started a tirade of abuse. Said I just lay cold to be contrary and probably accused her of hiding it. . . . I believe she doesn't like it that I entertain this club [the A Volonte club] as the same thing happens every time my time comes to entertain. Before we start a new year in it next fall, shall ask her if she objects to my belonging to it.

August 27, 1909

. . . Mr. Stableton [her superintendent of schools] telephoned. . . . Wanted to talk to me about changing my grade. . . . Said it was a hard room so was not going to make me take it.

Said I should tell and talk it over with my folks. . . . Mr. L [J. B. Lennon] said I should not take it. . . .

September 11, 1910
. . . Mrs. L acted very sharp. . . . Think she gets angry when I go to the Unitarian. . . .

June 22, 1913
. . . Started to dust the dining room when Mr. L fairly flew at me for working—had told me before I ought to rest . . . talked horrid—broke me up for the rest of the day. Do the best I can and his scolding was uncalled for. . . .

August 10, 1913
. . . Myra [a fellow teacher] told me the Board had placed me in 6A Edwards School. Mrs. L and Mrs. Reed next door were on way to high school by 8:30AM to protest, but got no satisfaction. . . .

November 10, 1914
. . . Mr. L wrote that Mrs. L had told him I thought of talking to Miss Van Buskirk about buying her out. Wrote a very discouraging letter—talked as though I'd be disgraced if I went into it [the beauty parlor business]. Wonder if was afraid I'd want to borrow money from them. Also asked me if I considered what effect it would have on my home relations. No doubt by that meant I wouldn't be there to do all the work. . . .

May 10, 1915
. . . Mrs. L grouchy—first time she's had to have some one clean house for about seven years. I've always done it before and after school. Guess she doesn't like to pay out $2.00 per day. . . .

July 21, 1915
. . . Rc'd letter from . . . Mrs. L. suggested my coming up to Chicago. . . . Don't think I'd care to go. . . .

March 23, 1916
Rc'd letter from Mrs. L asking me to come East. Thinks I need a rest.

March 24, 1916
. . . wrote to folks this AM. I wouldn't come East. Didn't want to lose my time at school.

May 19, 1919
. . . Had short visit with Mr. J. K. [superintendent of schools Stableton]. Thinks it's my duty to keep house for Mr. L.

June 4, 1919
. . . letter from "father"—Is very lonesome.

August 4, 1919
. . . Nelle Clancy . . . came to take me for a ride . . . returned about 10:15. Got the most awfulest scoring I'd ever received from anyone. Had been up at Clancy's and spoke of calling up the police to find us. The most unjust thing I've ever had done to me. . . .

October 12, 1921

. . . Woman's Club meeting . . . didn't get home until five. Mr. L worried because I was out so long tho Duncan slept most of the time. Seems I can't go anywhere in peace. . . .

October 19, 1921

Would like to have heard Prof. Beyer . . . but Mr. L went down town early so I had to stay in. . . .

November 28, 1922

. . . Club met. . . . Had planned to go but Mr. L started to act up again. Is so selfish.

April 10, 1923

. . . Concert at Normal Lecture Course but no one to stay with D.

October 24, 1923

. . . Got started for P[ontiac] at 2:40. D soon went to sleep. . . . Don't enjoy going everywhere alone. . . .

DOCUMENT SET 3: STUDENT

EXCERPT FROM THE CURRICULUM REQUIREMENTS FOR THE "72 WEEK PROGRAM IN HOME ECONOMICS" AS LISTED IN THE *ISNU NORMAL SCHOOL QUARTERLY CONTAINING THE SIXTY-EIGHTH ANNUAL CATALOG, APRIL 1926.* (ORIGINAL SPELLING IS RETAINED AND REFLECTS THE SIMPLIFIED SPELLING TREND THAT ISNU ENDORSED DURING THE EARLY DECADES OF THE TWENTIETH CENTURY.)

Dr. Joanne Rayfield Archives, Milner Library, Illinois State University, http://library. illinoisstate.edu/unique-collections/archives/catalogsmain.php

FIRST YEAR

FALL	WINTER	SPRING
Beginning clothing 31	Garment Making 32	Dressmaking 33
Cooking 31	Cooking 32	Household M'g't 33
Textils	Teaching Process	Psychology 33
Design	Drawing 1	Color 35
Physical Training	Physical Training	Physical Training

SECOND YEAR

FALL	WINTER	SPRING
Home Econ. Org 43	Advanst Dressmaking	Economics 31
Physiology 31	Home Nursing	*Public Speaking
Dress Design or	School Management	Science of Discourse
Experimental Cookery	Teaching	Teaching
General Method 34		

DOCUMENT SET 4: UNION ACTIVISM

EXCERPTS FROM THE *PANTAGRAPH'S* COVERAGE OF THE BFT DURING ITS
FORMATIVE MONTHS IN 1934

Milner Library, Illinois State University, Normal

February 28, 1934

The Bloomington Federation of Teachers, with a membership of 100 school teachers, has
been fully organized . . . according to an announcement by J. P. Harrison, Bloomington high
school teacher, president of the organization. The other officers are Mrs. Barbara Lennon,
vice-president. . . . The objects of the federation . . . are: "to bring teachers into relations of
mutual assistance and co-operation. . . . [And] To co-operate with the parent-teacher association, the board of education, and such officials in matters of mutual concern." Since the
beginning of the organization a few weeks ago the membership has increased every week. . . .

March 6, 1934

Schools should continue next year only so long as there are funds for operation, according
to the Bloomington Federation of Teachers, No. 276. The opinion was contained in a letter
to the board of education from the executive council. . . . The letter said: " . . . The executive council of the federation wished to take this opportunity to assure the board of its
hearty cooperation in all matters relating to the welfare of schools. In view of this . . . the
Bloomington Federation respectfully submits the following recommendations: That schools
operate nine months this year . . . with all salaries paid in cash. . . . That schools operate next
year, 1934–35 only as long as funds permit. In case funds for 1934–35 are insufficient, we
recommend that schools be closed as soon as funds are exhausted and be kept closed until
adequate financial provision is made. . . . "

DOCUMENT SET 5: POLITICAL ACTIVISM

EXCERPTS FROM THE WTUL NEWSLETTER'S ANNOUNCEMENTS REGARDING
EQUALITY ISSUES

Bulletin (WTUL, Chicago), George A. Smathers Libraries, University of Florida, http://ufdc.ufl.edu/UF00089422/

VOL. 38, NO. 10 (OCTOBER 1946)

"Equal Rights Amendment Defeated"
Near the close of the 79th Congress, the so-called "Equal Rights" Amendment was defeated. . . . This Amendment, as you know, if adopted, would destroy the labor laws and other protective legislation for women. . . . We still have to be on guard to see that the new candidates for Congress are not misled by the term "equal rights. . . . " Let us see that the candidates are informed as to the dangers of this blanket legislation.

VOL. 39, NOs. 2–3 (MARCH 1947)

"New Proposal on the Legal Status of Women"
. . . The purpose of this Bill is to present a practicable working program for the elimination of unfair legal discriminations against women. . . . This Bill represents a positive program but is not an amendment such as the Equal Rights that we have been opposing for so many years. It is in the form of a Resolution . . . stating that . . . in law and its administration, no distinctions on the basis of sex shall be made except those reasonably based on differences in physical structure, biological or social function.

VOL. 39, NO. 7 (JULY 1947)

"Federal Equal Pay Bill Introduced"
. . . The campaign for the Equal Pay legislation will now shift to Congress and this will be one of the major bills the women's organizations will work for.

VOL. 41, NO. 4 (APRIL 1949)

"Equal Pay Bill"
. . . This bill would abolish discrimination between sexes in the payment of wages and require penalties for violation. . . .

ABBREVIATIONS

ACLU	American Civil Liberties Union
AFL	American Federation of Labor
AFT	American Federation of Teachers
AWL	American Women's League
BELF	Barbara Egger Lennon File Folders in Barbara Egger Lennon Collection
BELJ	Barbara Egger Lennon Journals in Barbara Egger Lennon Collection
BELSB	Barbara Egger Lennon Scrapbooks in Barbara Egger Lennon Collection
BFT	Bloomington Federation of Teachers
BHS	Bloomington High School
BTLA	Bloomington Trades and Labor Assembly
CFT	Chicago Federation of Teachers
CIO	Congress of Industrial Organizations
CLL	Civil Liberties League
DAR	Daughters of the American Revolution

ERA	Equal Rights Amendment
IDW	Illinois Democratic Women
IEA	Illinois Education Association
IFL	Illinois Federation of Labor
IFT	Illinois Federation of Teachers
ISNU	Illinois State Normal University
ISTA	Illinois State Teachers Association (original name of IEA)
JBL	John Brown Lennon
JBLC	John Brown Lennon Collection
JTU	Journeyman Tailors Union
MCHM	McLean County History Museum
NEA	National Education Association
WCTU	Women's Christian Temperance Union
WTUL	Women's Trade Union League
YWCA	Young Women's Christian Association

STUDY QUESTIONS

1. The author uses the term *social housekeeping* to describe Juna's and Barbe's efforts at public activism in the decades before the Great Depression. What is meant by that term? What sorts of activism fell within its boundaries? How could participation both reinforce and counter traditional ideas about women's proper roles?
2. Why and how did women's roles as students and educators alter from the late nineteenth to the early twentieth century? How could this shift both reinforce and counter traditional ideas about women's proper roles?
3. How did Barbe's post-1932 union and labor activism differ from her pre-Depression activism? In what ways were they similar?
4. Throughout much of Barbe's life, she contends with her multiple responsibilities as a family member, a working woman, and a social activist. How does this struggle to balance competing roles compare to traditional views of women's roles in the first half of the twentieth century?
5. Neither Barbe nor the author describes Barbara Egger Lennon as a "feminist." Do you think that label would be an accurate one? Why or why not?

PRIMARY SOURCE STUDY QUESTIONS

1. Chapter 2 addresses the ways in which Barbe's life often was governed by deference to authority figures. What does the Primary Sources Document Set 1 tell you about the ways in which her teaching career contributed to this deferential construct? Do these documents offer any evidence that her teaching experience could help build a sense of independence?
2. Chapters 2–6 discuss Barbe's ongoing and evolving struggle to establish a sense of autonomy while also fulfilling her expected roles as a family member. What do the journal entries in Primary Sources Document Set 2 tell you about her success or failure in those attempts? How do these entries support or challenge your understanding of women's traditional roles (as daughter, wife, mother) during the first two decades of the twentieth century?
3. Chapters 4 and 6 address the competing arguments about the potential effects of domestic science and home economic programs. What were those arguments, and how do the home economics degree requirements (Primary Source Document Set 3) illustrate facets of this argument?
4. Chapter 7 discusses the Depression-era rise of teachers' unions like the Bloomington Federation of Teachers. How did 1930s federal legislation affect this growth? How did the preponderance of female membership in teachers' unions affect public perception regarding their rights? How

did the BFT's early endeavors (as reported by the newspaper articles in Primary Source Document Set 4) illustrate the potential strengths and challenges faced by teachers' organizations?

5. In the decades after the Nineteenth Amendment was ratified, the fight over the ERA split the activist community. What does the 1947 WTUL newsletter coverage of this topic (Primary Source Document Set 5) tell you about how female labor activists viewed the ERA? What was the basis for their opinion? Do you think that their viewpoint had more validity for the time period than their opposition? Why or why not?

NOTES

CHAPTER 1: FROM STUDENT TO TEACHER, 1880s–1902

1. *Pantagraph,* June 21, 1900.
2. Barbe's age cannot be definitively stated. Evidence (early census data, vital records, journal entries, and family history) indicates that Barbara K. Egger was born in Switzerland in 1881 and traveled to the United States in 1883 with her mother and siblings. This 1881 birth date is supported by the 1900 US Census, which reports her birth month and year as May 1881 as well as her own journal entry dated May 18, 1906, in which Barbe notes her birthday and describes the gifts she received. By September 1910, however, she had begun to make note of her birthday on September 18 of each year, and census records from 1910 on as well as future vital records (such as the Social Security Index) show her birth date and place as September 18, 1884, in Switzerland. This September 1884 Swiss birth seems unlikely, given the fact that her parents were both settled in Illinois by this date. Steamship travel had made the transatlantic crossing much more manageable. Nevertheless, regardless of the relative ease and common occurrence of multiple ocean crossings, no proof of any return trips by her mother could be located. Weighing the evidence lends itself to the conclusion that she was born in May 1881 in Switzerland and for reasons unclear adopted the later date.
3. BELJ, August 30, 1906, August 19, 1908, May 9, 1906.
4. *Chicago Chronicle,* January 29, 1901.
5. Handwritten letters of recommendation for Barbara Egger from D. T. Foster and J. B. Lennon to Bloomington school superintendent John Wren, 1902, in BELF.

CHAPTER 2: PERSONAL AND PROFESSIONAL DEFERENCE TO AUTHORITY, 1902–1908

1. Barbara Egger, handwritten shower invitation, September 8, 1905, in BELSB.
2. BELJ, May 2, 1905.
3. *Pantagraph,* January 8, 1908; Admiral F. E. Chadwick, "The Woman Peril in American Education," *Educational Review* (1914), as quoted in Kathleen Weiler, *Country Schoolwomen: Teaching in Rural California, 1850–1950* (Stanford, CA: Stanford University Press, 1998), 24.
4. BELJ, October 23, 1905, May 11, 1906.
5. "The Justrite Vacuum Cleaner" advertisement, ca. 1910, original available at the MCHM.
6. BELJ, December 18, 1907, May 9, 1906, October 28, 1907.

7. BELJ, October 3, 1908.
8. *YWCA,* ca. 1908, in BELSB.

CHAPTER 3: ASPIRING NEW WOMAN, 1909–1915

1. BELJ, October 11, 1911.
2. BELJ, March 3, 11, April 8, 1914.
3. BELJ, December 14, 15, 1914.
4. BELJ, January 13, 14, 23, 24, 1915.
5. BELJ, January 28, 1915.
6. BELJ, February 21, 1915.
7. BELJ, March 17, 29, April 4, 1915.
8. BELJ, April 20, 1915.

CHAPTER 4: NEW WOMAN, 1915–1918

1. David Felmley as quoted in John B. Freed, *Educating Illinois: Illinois State University, 1857–2007* (Virginia Beach: Donning, 2009), 197.
2. BELJ, September 11, 1916.
3. BELJ, March 10, 11, 1917.
4. BELJ, July 2, 1917.
5. BELJ, October 2, 1918.

CHAPTER 5: FROM NEW WOMAN AT WORK TO NEW WOMAN AT HOME, 1919–1921

1. BELJ, May 6, 8, 1919.
2. BELJ, July 26, 1919; JBL expense log notebook, 1918–1920, in JBLC.
3. BELJ, June 9, 1920; James Duncan to JBL, July 17, 1919, in JBLC.
4. BELJ, August 5, 1919.
5. BELJ, May 4, 1920.
6. BELJ, June 9, 1920.
7. Handwritten letter from J. K. Stableton to JBL and Barbe, July 28, 1920, in BELSB.
8. BELJ, September 17, 1920.

CHAPTER 6: MOTHERHOOD AND THE NEW WOMAN, 1921–1928

1. JBL, "Last Will and Testament," January 22, 1922, original available in BELF.
2. BELJ, October 12, 1921.
3. BELJ, June 24, 1908.
4. BELJ, August 10, 1912.
5. BELJ, March 12, October 8, 1923.
6. Bertha Strickler, "The Principles of Scientific Corset Fitting," in *An Intimate Affair: Women, Lingerie, and Sexuality,* edited by Jill Fields (Berkeley: University of California Press, 1987), 64.
7. BELJ, June 7, 1928.

CHAPTER 7: UNION ORGANIZING AND LOCAL POLITICS, 1929–1937

1. BELJ, March 8, 1932; *Pantagraph,* March 25, 1932.
2. BELJ, September 15, October 7, 1932.
3. BELJ, November 24, 1932.
4. BFT's "Statement of Purpose" in the *Pantagraph,* February 28, 1934.
5. BELJ, May 2, 1934, March 14, 1935.
6. *Pantagraph,* March 23, 1935.

CHAPTER 8: FROM LOCAL ORGANIZER TO NATIONAL REFORMER, 1937–1945

1. BELJ, July 13, 1926.
2. CLL "Constitution" in the *Pantagraph,* May 4, 1939.
3. BELJ, December 11, 1940, June 29, 1941.
4. BELJ, October 11, 1940.
5. BELJ, September 21, 1941.

CHAPTER 9: POLITICAL BATTLES WON AND LOST, 1945–1950

1. BELJ, August 14, 1945.
2. BELJ, April 12, June 6, 1949.
3. *Bulletin* (WTUL, Chicago) 38 (October 1946), George A. Smathers Libraries, University of Florida, http://ufdc.ufl.edu/UF00089422/.
4. BELJ, November 5, 1947.
5. *Bulletin* (WTUL, Chicago) 40 (March 1948).
6. BELJ, June 18, 1950.

CHAPTER 10: CONTINUITY AND CHANGE, 1950–1983

1. BELJ, June 2, 26, 1953.

ANNOTATED BIBLIOGRAPHY

PRIMARY SOURCES

Prior to this biography, nothing had been written on Barbara Egger Lennon's life, so this work has been constructed from the ground up. The Barbara Egger Lennon Collection, which is held at the archives of the McLean County History Museum in Bloomington, Illinois, provided a strong foundation on which to reconstruct her story. It contains nearly seventy years of her daily journals (BELJ) as well as numerous scrapbooks (BELSB) and file folders (BELF) full of personal and professional records as well as memorabilia and photos. The John Brown Lennon Collection, which is also held in the archives of the MCHM, helped fill in cracks in that foundation. In addition to the exampled sources offered in the "Primary Sources" section, other helpful published primary sources included *Bloomington City Directories;* the *Aegis; McLean County Schools Newsletter;* ISNU's yearbook, *The Index; Bloomington Public Schools: We Grow, a Report of Progress, 1944–1955* (all of which are available at the MCHM); as well as the widely available United States Census and vital records such as birth and death available via the Illinois Regional Archives Depositories.

SECONDARY SOURCES

This book focuses on Barbara Egger Lennon's experiences as a family member, an educator, and an activist. In many chapters, these themes intertwine, and all three themes cross from one chapter to the next. As such it is difficult to separate supporting secondary source material by chapter. The same holds true for the main themes, as many authors address these same multiple facets in their work. Nonetheless, what follows is an attempt to do the latter by providing a brief and selective list of secondary source material divided by major themes. Works that address multiple themes are categorized within the theme in which they best applied for this work.

Family: For discussions regarding practical facets of Barbe's shifting roles as daughter, wife, and mother as well as general information regarding women's lives and societal expectations during varying time spans, see the following: Dorothy Brown, *Setting a Course: American Women in the 1920s* (Boston: Twayne, 1987); Stephanie Coontz, *Marriage, a History: From Obedience to Intimacy; or, How Love Conquered Marriage* (New York: Viking, 2005) and *The Way We Never Were: American Families and the Nostalgia Trap* (New York: Basic Books, 1992); Ruth Schwartz Cowan, *More Work for Mother: The Ironies of Household*

Technology from the Open Hearth to the Microwave (New York: Basic Books, 1983); Rochelle Gatlin, *American Women Since 1945* (Jackson: University Press of Mississippi, 1987); Linda Gordon, *Pitied but Not Entitled: Single Mothers and the History of Welfare, 1890–1935* (New York: Free Press, 1994); Jean V. Matthews, *The Rise of the New Woman: The Women's Movement in America, 1875–1930* (Chicago: Ivan R. Dee, 2003); Joanne J. Meyerowitz, *Women Adrift: Independent Wage Earners in Chicago, 1880–1930* (Chicago: University of Chicago Press, 1988); Carolyn M. Moehling, *Mothers' Pensions Legislation and the Cross-state Variation in Welfare Generosity*, presented at the Economic History Association, August 2006, http://eh.net/eha/system/files/eha-meeting-2006/pdf/session_3b_moehling.pdf; Rebecca Jo Plant, *Mom: The Transformation of Motherhood in Modern America* (Chicago: University of Chicago Press, 2010); Rosalind Rosenberg, *Divided Lives: American Women in the Twentieth Century* (New York: Hill & Wang, 1992); Linda W. Rosenzweig, "'The Anchor of My Life': Middle-Class American Mothers and College Educated Daughters, 1880–1920," in *Family & Society in American History*, edited by Joseph M. Hawes and Elizabeth I. Nybakken (Urbana: University of Illinois Press, 2001); Dorothy Schneider and Carl J. Schneider, *American Women in the Progressive Era, 1900–1920* (New York: Facts on File, 1993); and Susan Ware, *Holding Their Own: American Women in the 1930s* (Boston: Twayne, 1982).

Teacher: Works used to ground Barbe's teaching career into a broader context include the following: William B. Brigham, *The Story of McLean County and Its Schools* (Bloomington, IL: William B. Brigham, 1951); Patricia A. Carter, *"Everybody's Paid but the Teacher": The Teaching Profession and the Women's Movement* (New York: Teachers College Press, 2002); Larry Cuban, *How Teachers Taught: Consistency and Change in Americans Classrooms, 1880–1990*, 2nd ed. (New York: Teachers College Press, 1993); June Edwards, *Women in American Education, 1820–1955: The Female Force and Educational Reform* (Westport, CT: Greenwood Press, 2002); Nancy Hoffman, *Woman's "True" Profession: Voices from the History of Teaching* (Cambridge, MA: Harvard Education Press, 2003); Dan Liefel, *Our Proud History: Bloomington Public Schools, District 87 Sesquicentennial, 1857–2007* (Bloomington, IL: Star Net Digital, 2007); Joel Perlmann and Robert A. Mango, *Women's Work? American School Teachers, 1650–1920* (Chicago: University of Chicago Press, 2001); Kate Rousmaniere, *City Teachers: Teaching and School Reform in Historical Perspective* (New York: Teachers College Press, 1997); and Kathleen Weiler, *Country Schoolwomen: Teaching in Rural California, 1850–1950* (Stanford, CA: Stanford University Press, 1998).

Student: Discussions that provide a wider context in which to frame Barbe's life as a student can be found in the following: Megan J. Elias, *Stir It Up: Home Economics in American Culture* (Philadelphia: University of Pennsylvania Press, 2008); John B. Freed, *Educating Illinois: Illinois State University, 1857–2007* (Virginia Beach: Donning, 2009); Monica Cousins Noraian, *Women's Rights, Racial Integration, and Education from 1850–1920: The Case of Sarah Raymond, the First Female Superintendent* (New York: Palgrave Macmillan, 2009); Barbara Miller Solomon, *In the Company of Educated Women: A History of Women in Higher Education in America* (New Haven, CT: Yale University Press, 1985); and Sarah Stage and Virginia B. Vincenti, eds., *Rethinking Home Economics: Women and the History of a Profession* (Ithaca, NY: Cornell University Press, 1997).

Union Activism: For information regarding union organizing and structure as well as general information regarding wage-earning women, see William Edward Eaton, *The American Federation of Teachers, 1916–1961: A History of the Movement* (Carbondale: Southern Illinois University Press, 1975); Alice Kessler-Harrison, *In Pursuit of Equity: Women, Men, and the Quest of Economic Citizenship in 20th-Century America* (New York: Oxford University Press, 2001) and *Out to Work: A History of Wage Earning Women in the United States* (New York: Oxford University Press, 1982); "Labor Unions in McLean County," http://www.

bntrades.org/; John F. Lyons, *Teachers and Reform: Chicago Public Education, 1929–1970* (Urbana: University of Illinois Press, 2008); Marjorie Murphy, *Blackboard Unions: The AFT and the NEA, 1900–1980* (Ithaca, NY: Cornell University Press, 1990); George Propeck and Irving F. Pearson, *The History of the Illinois Education Association: Its Influence upon the Development of Public Education with the State* (Springfield: Illinois Education Association, 1961); Robert L. Reid, ed., *Battle Ground: The Autobiography of Margaret Haley* (Urbana: University of Illinois Press, 1982); Wayne J. Urban, *Gender, Race, and the National Education Association: Professionalism and Its Limits* (New York: Routledge Falmer, 2000); and Barbara Mayer Wertheimer, *We Were There: The Story of Working Women in America* (New York: Pantheon Books, 1977).

Political Activism: Further discussions regarding reform efforts from social housekeeping to political lobbying can be found in the following: "The American Woman's League and the American Woman's Republic," University City Public Library, http://history.ucpl.lib.mo.us/awlawrc.asp; Roger Biles, *Crusading Liberal: Paul H. Douglas of Illinois* (DeKalb: Northern Illinois University Press, 2002); Dorothy Sue Cobble, *The Other Woman's Movement: Workplace Justice and Social Rights in Modern America* (Princeton, NJ: Princeton University Press, 2004); Eleanor Flexner and Ellen Fitzpatrick, *Century of Struggle: The Woman's Rights Movement in the United States,* 3rd ed. (Cambridge, MA: Harvard University Press, 1996); J. Stanley Lemons, *The Woman Citizen: Social Feminism in the 1920s* (Urbana: University of Illinois Press, 1973); Charles J. Masters, *Governor Henry Horner, Chicago Politics and the Great Depression* (Carbondale: Southern Illinois University Press, 2007); Robyn Muncy, *Creating a Female Dominion in American Reform, 1890–1935* (New York: Oxford University Press, 1991); Agnes Nestor, *Woman's Labor Leader: An Autobiography of Agnes Nestor* (Rockford, IL: Bellevue Books, 1954); and Elizabeth Anne Payne, *Reform, Labor, and Feminism: Margaret Dreier Robins and the Women's Trade Union League* (Urbana: University of Illinois Press, 1988).

INDEX

Soviet Union, 150–151
Spanish influenza, 68–70
Spencer Corset Company, 103–104
Standards of education, 21–24
Status of Women bill, 161
Stevenson, Adlai, 159–161, 166
Stock market crash (1929), 90, 107–109
Stoddard, John L., 14
Strikes, labor, 130, 134, 145
Suffrage, female, 13, 33–36, 38, 60, 71, 131
Sunday, Billy, 29–30, 39
Swanish, Peter, 136
Swiss immigrant community, 6–8

Taft, William Howard, 40
Taft-Hartley Act (1947), 156–157
Tax revenues
  funding Depression-era education, 113–116, 118
  property taxes funding Bloomington schools, 107–108
  school taxation limits, 143–144
  union involvement, 122–123
  war economy reducing opposition to higher school taxes, 144–145
Taxpayers Protection League, 112, 122–123
Teacher training, 52–55, 59, 61–62, 105–107. *See also* Illinois State Normal University
Teaching
  Barbe leaving Bloomington, 44–45
  Barbe's national reform efforts, 129–130
  Barbe's retirement from, 162, 164
  Barbe's return to Bloomington, 19–20, 22–24
  Barbe's tenure as principal of Sarah Raymond School, 68–69
  expanding programs in the 1920s, 106
  Great Depression in Bloomington, 111–113, 116–117
  Hopedale, Illinois, 17–20
  increasing number of women in, 20–21
  organizing local teachers, 120–124
  overriding marriage offers, 66–67
  pension protection fight, 72–73
  professional growth, 42

psychic prognostication, 45
return after ISNU training, 63
substitute teaching, 86–87
See also Education
Temperance, 30–31, 44, 67
Tenure protection for teachers, 114, 120, 137–138, 143–145, 147
Thurmond, Strom, 160
To Secure These Rights (civil rights report), 158–159
Travis, Billie, 66–67, 72
Truman, Bess, 157
Truman, Harry, 155, 159, 161

Unions
  anticommunist efforts to control curriculum, 138–139
  Barbe's AFT involvement, 117–120
  Barbe's membership in teachers' associations, 72–73, 87
  Bloomington schools' increasing demands on teachers without increasing salaries, 157–158
  conservative movement threatening, 71–72
  J. B.'s background of activism, 12–13
  J. B.'s declining influence with age, 92
  liberalism of the AFT, 133–136
  local election victories, 116
  NEA response to Great Depression funding, 117
  postwar rightward political swing, 155–156
  real estate assessment referendum, 145
  Taft-Hartley Act, 156–157
  tax referendum and salary increase, 144
  teachers' unions, 117–124
  women's labor rights, 130
  World War II efforts, 147
Unit Bill, 143–146
Unitarian Church
  Barbe's early interest in, 44–45
  Barbe's growing social life, 56, 72, 85
  Barbe's interest in racial equality, 132, 140–141
  Barbe's retirement activities, 165
  Erdmann's marriage, 50–51
  evangelicals' criticism of, 29–30
  pragmatic liberalism, 139

CPSIA information can be obtained at www.ICGtesting.com
Printed in the USA
LVOW04s1201021214

416682LV00001B/1/P